W9-APV-867

CHICKEN COOKBOOK

EDITOR: Maryanne Blacker
FOOD EDITOR: Pamela Clark

∎ ∎ ∎

ART DIRECTOR: Paula Wooller
DESIGNER: Robbylee Phelan

∎ ∎ ∎

DEPUTY FOOD EDITOR: Jan Castorina
ASSISTANT FOOD EDITOR: Kathy Snowball
ASSOCIATE FOOD EDITOR: Enid Morrison
CHIEF HOME ECONOMIST: Kathy Wharton
DEPUTY CHIEF HOME ECONOMIST: Louise Patniotis
HOME ECONOMISTS: Tracey Port, Quinton Kohler, Jill Lange, Voula Mantzouridis, Alexandra McCowan, Kathy McGarry, Dimitra Stais
EDITORIAL COORDINATOR: Elizabeth Hooper
KITCHEN ASSISTANT: Amy Wong

∎ ∎ ∎

STYLISTS: Marie-Helene Clauzon, Rosemary de Santis, Carolyn Fienberg, Jacqui Hing, Michelle Gorry
PHOTOGRAPHERS: Kevin Brown, Robert Clark, Robert Taylor, Jon Waddy

∎ ∎ ∎

HOME LIBRARY STAFF

ASSISTANT EDITOR: Beverley Hudec
EDITORIAL COORDINATOR: Fiona Nicholas

∎ ∎ ∎

PUBLISHER: Richard Walsh
DEPUTY PUBLISHER: Nick Chan

∎ ∎ ∎

Produced by The Australian Women's Weekly Home Library. Typeset by ACP Colour Graphics Pty Ltd. Printed by Dai Nippon Co., Ltd in Japan.
Published by ACP Publishing Pty Ltd, 54 Park Street, Sydney.

♦ U.S.A.: Distributed for Whitecap Books Ltd. by Graphic Arts Center Publishing, 3019 N.W. Yeon, Portland, OR, 97210. Tel: 503-226-2402. Fax: 503-223-1410
♦ CANADA: Distributed in Canada by Whitecap Books Ltd, 1086 West 3rd St, North Vancouver B.C V7P 3J6. Tel: 604-980-9852. Fax: 604-980-8197

∎ ∎ ∎

Chicken Cookbook
ISBN 1 86396 005 8

∎ ∎ ∎

© A C P Publishing Pty Ltd 1993
ACN 053 273 546

∎ ∎ ∎

With our recipes, chicken is tasty and tempting as never before, and you'll serve success every time because it's so popular! Other favorites, turkey, duck and goose are all here, as are quail and pheasant, now widely available. Serving sizes are very much up to what you think people will eat, so our serving suggestions can be varied to suit their appetites. Where there are tricky things to do, we show you in step-by-step pictures with individual recipes. Also see "Pre-Cooking Preparations" at the back of this book for simple procedures for best results, plus a guide to the cuts we bought, and cooking and microwaving tips.

Pamela Clark
FOOD EDITOR

COVER: From top: Mustard Chicken Pie, page 71, Chili and Lemon Grass Rock Cornish Hens, page 106.
OPPOSITE: Stir-Fried Chicken and Ginger Noodles, Chicken Satay Flan, page 48.
INSIDE BACK COVER: Sesame Chicken and Mandarin Salad, Cassoulet of Quail with Thyme and Lentils, page 76.
BACK COVER: Turkey Breast Roll with Fresh Tomato Relish, page 91.

SOUPS

Slowly, the delicious aromas will intensify until the soup you are cooking becomes irresistible – and your bonus is not only flavor, but the goodness of fresh ingredients, particularly vegetables. Recipes range from light to hearty, with most based on chicken, plus quail and duck for variety. There's the contrast of cream-style soups and broths (one with tasty chicken meatballs), hearty minestrone and Oriental inventions such as ginger chicken gow gees in sherried broth. For a good crunch, try spicy garlic bread or baked garlic croutons, each an accompaniment to its own recipe.

PANCETTA AND CHICKEN BROTH WITH GNOCCHI

2½ tablespoons olive oil
½lb boneless, skinless
    chicken breasts
10 cups water
3 large chicken bouillon
    cubes, crumbled
2 leeks, sliced
1½ tablespoons chopped
    fresh chives
8 slices pancetta, chopped

GNOCCHI
⅓ bunch (7oz) spinach
½lb sweet potato, chopped
1 teaspoon butter
1 egg yolk
⅓ cup grated pecorino cheese
¾ cup all-purpose flour,
    approximately

Heat oil in pan, add chicken, cook until browned all over and tender; slice finely.

Combine water and bouillon cubes in large pan, bring to boil, add chicken and leeks, simmer, uncovered, 15 minutes.
Just before serving, add gnocchi, chives and pancetta to pan, simmer, uncovered, 7 minutes or until gnocchi rise to surface.
Gnocchi: Boil, steam or microwave spinach until tender, drain, chop finely; squeeze out excess moisture. Boil, steam or microwave sweet potato until soft, mash well. Stir in spinach, butter, egg yolk and cheese; mix well. Stir in enough sifted flour to form a soft dough, cover; refrigerate 30 minutes. Shape 1 level teaspoon of mixture into an oval; repeat with remaining mixture.

Serves 6.

■ Broth can be prepared a day ahead. Gnocchi can be made 6 hours ahead.
■ Storage: Covered, in refrigerator.
■ Freeze: Uncooked gnocchi suitable.
■ Microwave: Vegetables suitable.

CURRIED SHRIMP AND CHICKEN SOUP

2½lb chicken
8 cups water
15 black peppercorns
1 onion, quartered
1 carrot, chopped
1 stalk celery, chopped
2 bay leaves
¼ teaspoon dried rosemary leaves
¼ teaspoon ground coriander
½ teaspoon turmeric
¼ teaspoon ground cumin
¼ teaspoon ground cardamom
½ teaspoon garam masala
12 cooked jumbo shrimp
¼ cup (½ stick) butter
⅓ cup all-purpose flour
1 cup (7oz) prunes
½ bunch (10oz) spinach, shredded

Combine chicken, water, peppercorns, onion, carrot, celery, herbs and spices in large pan. Bring to boil, simmer, covered, 1½ hours. Remove chicken, strain broth into bowl, discard onion mixture. Return chicken to broth, cool, cover, refrigerate several hours or overnight.

Next day, skim fat from broth, remove chicken from broth, remove skin from chicken, remove meat from bones, discard skin and bones; chop chicken meat.

Shell and devein half the shrimp, leaving heads and tails intact. Shell and devein remaining shrimp completely, chop finely.

Melt butter in large pan, stir in flour, cook until bubbling. Remove from heat, gradually stir in broth. Stir over heat until mixture boils and thickens. Add prunes, chicken meat and chopped shrimp, stir until heated through.

Just before serving, stir in spinach. Serve soup with remaining shrimp.

Serves 6.

■ Recipe can be prepared a day ahead.
■ Storage: Covered, in refrigerator.
■ Freeze: Suitable.
■ Microwave: Not suitable.

LEFT; Pancetta and Chicken Broth with Gnocchi.
ABOVE: Curried Shrimp and Chicken Soup.

CHICKEN AND BROCCOLI SOUP

1lb chicken thigh cutlets
1 potato, chopped
1 onion, chopped
2 bay leaves
6 large fresh basil leaves
4 cups water
2½ tablespoons butter
¼ cup all-purpose flour
1 small chicken bouillon
    cube, crumbled
⅓ cup sour cream
½lb broccoli stems, chopped
2 green onions, chopped
1½ tablespoons chopped fresh chives

Combine chicken, potato, onion, bay and basil leaves and water in pan, bring to boil, simmer, covered, 30 minutes. Strain mixture, reserve chicken, broth and vegetables separately; discard leaves. Remove meat from bones, discard skin and bones; chop meat finely.

Melt butter in large pan, stir in flour, stir over heat until bubbling. Remove from heat, gradually stir in reserved broth. Stir over heat until mixture boils and thickens. Blend or process half the mixture with reserved vegetables until smooth. Add bouillon cube and sour cream, blend until combined, return mixture to pan with the chicken meat.

Combine remaining soup mixture with broccoli and green onions in pan. Bring to boil, simmer, covered, about 5 minutes or until broccoli is soft. Blend or process mixture until smooth, return to pan; add chives.

Heat soup mixtures separately without boiling, pour into 2 jugs, pour simultaneously into serving bowls.

Serves 6.

■ Recipe can be made 6 hours ahead.
■ Storage: Covered, in refrigerator.
■ Freeze: Not suitable.
■ Microwave: Suitable.

CHICKEN MEATBALLS IN LIGHT VEGETABLE BROTH

¾lb ground chicken
1 egg, lightly beaten
¼ cup seasoned stuffing mix
2½ tablespoons chopped
    fresh parsley
oil for deep-frying
1 carrot
2 stalks celery
6 cups water
2 green onions, chopped
1 large chicken bouillon cube, crumbled
1½ tablespoons light soy sauce

Combine chicken, egg, stuffing mix and parsley in bowl. Using lightly floured hands, roll 1 rounded tablespoon of mixture into a ball; repeat with remaining mixture. Deep-fry chicken meatballs in batches in hot oil until lightly browned and cooked through; drain on absorbent paper.

Cut carrot and celery into thin strips. Combine carrot, celery, water, onions, bouillon cube and sauce in pan. Bring to boil, add chicken meatballs, simmer, uncovered, about 5 minutes or until chicken meatballs are heated through.

Serves 4.

■ Soup can be prepared 2 days ahead.
■ Storage: Covered, in refrigerator.
■ Freeze: Not suitable.
■ Microwave: Suitable.

MINTED ASPARAGUS AND CHICKEN CREAM SOUP

2½lb chicken, quartered
8 cups water
1 large onion, quartered
1 stalk celery, chopped
¼ cup chopped flat-leafed parsley
1 large carrot, chopped
1 teaspoon black peppercorns
1 carrot, extra
2½ tablespoons butter
¼ cup all-purpose flour
2 small chicken bouillon
    cubes, crumbled
1 bunch (½lb) fresh asparagus,
    chopped
½ cup sour cream
1 egg, lightly beaten
2½ tablespoons tomato paste
1 tablespoon chopped fresh mint

Combine chicken, water, onion, celery, parsley, carrot and peppercorns in large pan. Bring to boil, simmer, covered, 1 hour; cool. Remove chicken, strain broth into large bowl; discard vegetables and peppercorns. Return chicken to broth, cover, refrigerate several hours or overnight.

Next day, skim fat from broth, remove chicken from broth, remove skin from chicken, remove meat from bones, discard skin and bones; cut meat into strips.

Cut extra carrot into thin strips. Heat butter in large pan, add carrot strips, cook, stirring, 5 minutes. Stir in flour, stir over heat until bubbling. Remove from heat, gradually stir in broth. Stir over heat until mixture boils and thickens, simmer, uncovered, 5 minutes. Add chicken meat, bouillon cubes and asparagus, simmer, uncovered, 5 minutes.

Combine sour cream, egg, paste and mint in bowl, beat until smooth. Stir into soup, stir until heated through; do not boil.

Serves 6.

■ Broth can be made 3 days ahead.
■ Storage: Covered, in refrigerator.
■ Freeze: Broth suitable.
■ Microwave: Soup suitable.

THAI-STYLE CHICKEN SOUP WITH SPICY GARLIC BREAD

1 tablespoon vegetable oil
1 leek, sliced
1 clove garlic, minced
1 teaspoon curry powder
1 teaspoon ground cumin
½ teaspoon ground coriander
1¼lb chicken thighs, boned,
    skinned, thinly sliced
4 cups water
3 small chicken bouillon
    cubes, crumbled
1 stalk lemon grass, halved
1½ cups canned unsweetened
    coconut milk
2 teaspoons sambal oelek
1 tablespoon cornstarch
1 tablespoon water, extra
1 teaspoon fish sauce
1 small red bell pepper, sliced
4 green onions, chopped
1 tablespoon lime juice
1 tablespoon chopped fresh cilantro

SPICY GARLIC BREAD
1 small bread stick
⅓ cup vegetable oil
1 tablespoon sambal oelek
¼ teaspoon garlic powder

Heat oil in pan, add leek and garlic, cook, stirring, until leek is soft. Stir in curry powder, cumin and coriander, cook, stirring, until fragrant. Add chicken, cook, stirring, until chicken is lightly browned.

Stir in water, bouillon cubes, lemon grass, coconut milk and sambal oelek. Bring to boil, simmer, uncovered, 10 minutes. Stir in blended cornstarch, extra water and fish sauce, stir until soup boils and thickens.

Just before serving, remove and discard lemon grass. Stir pepper, onions, juice and cilantro into soup. Serve soup with spicy garlic bread.

Spicy Garlic Bread: Cut bread stick into ½ inch slices. Brush slices on each side with combined oil, sambal oelek and garlic powder. Place slices in single layer on baking sheet. Bake in 350°F oven 5 minutes, turn bread, bake further 5 minutes or until crisp.

Serves 4.

■ Recipe can be made a day ahead.
■ Storage: Soup, covered, in
    refrigerator. Bread, in airtight
    container.
■ Freeze: Not suitable.
■ Microwave: Soup suitable.

LEFT: Clockwise from left: Chicken Meatballs in Light Vegetable Broth, Chicken and Broccoli Soup, Minted Asparagus and Chicken Cream Soup.
BELOW: Thai-Style Chicken Soup with Spicy Garlic Bread.

CHICKEN MINESTRONE

2 tablespoons (¼ stick) butter
1¼lb chicken thighs, boned,
   skinned, chopped
1 onion, sliced
1 clove garlic, minced
¼lb slices bacon, chopped
1 stalk celery, chopped
1 carrot, chopped
14½oz can tomatoes
8oz can red kidney beans,
   rinsed, drained
3 cups water
1 small chicken bouillon
   cube, crumbled
⅓ cup small pasta
2½ tablespoons chopped
   fresh oregano
1 tablespoon chopped fresh parsley

Heat butter in pan, add chicken, onion, garlic and bacon. Cook, stirring, until chicken is almost cooked. Stir in celery and carrot, cook, stirring, 5 minutes.

Stir in undrained crushed tomatoes, beans, water, bouillon cube and pasta. Bring to boil, simmer, uncovered, about 30 minutes or until minestrone is slightly thickened. Stir in herbs, simmer, uncovered, 5 minutes.

Serves 4.

■ Minestrone can be made a
  day ahead.
■ Storage: Covered, in refrigerator.
■ Freeze: Suitable.
■ Microwave: Suitable.

CHICKEN SPINACH CHOWDER WITH GARLIC CROUTONS

1 tablespoon vegetable oil
1 onion, chopped
1 clove garlic, minced
1¼lb chicken thighs, boned,
   skinned, chopped
2 medium potatoes, chopped
3 small chicken bouillon
   cubes, crumbled
4 cups water
¾ cup half-and-half
½ bunch (10oz) spinach, shredded

GARLIC CROUTONS
6 slices bread
¼ cup (½ stick) butter
2½ tablespoons vegetable oil
4 cloves garlic, minced
½ teaspoon garlic salt

Heat oil in pan, add onion and garlic, cook, stirring, until onion is soft. Add chicken, cook, stirring, until chicken is lightly browned and almost cooked.

Stir in potatoes, bouillon cubes and water; bring to boil, simmer, uncovered, about 10 minutes or until potatoes are soft. Stir in half-and-half and spinach, stir until heated through. Serve chowder with garlic croutons.

Garlic Croutons: Remove crusts from bread, cut bread into ½ inch cubes. Combine butter, oil, garlic and salt in bowl, add bread cubes, toss well. Place cubes evenly on baking sheet, bake in 375°F oven about 15 minutes or until lightly browned and crisp.

Serves 4.

■ Chowder best made close to serving.
  Croutons can be made several hours
  ahead, reheat in oven.
■ Freeze: Not suitable.
■ Microwave: Chowder suitable.

HOT AND SOUR SOUP

½ cup black fungus
1oz Chinese dried mushrooms
1½ tablespoons Chinese rice wine
3 cups water
2 small chicken bouillon
  cubes, crumbled
1 carrot, sliced
1 small fresh red chili pepper,
  finely chopped
2 teaspoons sugar
¼ cup white vinegar
1½ tablespoons light soy sauce
½lb boneless, skinless chicken
  breasts, thinly sliced
3 green onions, sliced

Place fungus and mushrooms in bowl, cover with boiling water, stand 20 minutes; drain. Chop fungus finely. Discard mushroom stems, slice mushroom caps.

Combine wine, water and bouillon cubes in pan, bring to boil, add fungus and mushrooms, carrot, chili, sugar, vinegar and sauce, simmer, uncovered, about 5 minutes or until carrot is tender. Add chicken and onions, simmer, uncovered, about 5 minutes or until chicken is tender.

Serves 4.

- Soup can be made 2 days ahead.
- Storage: Covered, in refrigerator.
- Freeze: Not suitable.
- Microwave: Suitable.

GINGER CHICKEN GOW GEES IN SHERRIED BROTH

½lb boneless, skinless
  chicken breasts
3 green onions, chopped
1 clove garlic, minced
1 teaspoon grated gingerroot
24 gow gees pastry sheets
1 teaspoon cornstarch
2 teaspoons water
2 tablespoons dry sherry
6 cups water, extra
¼ Chinese cabbage, shredded
1 large chicken bouillon
  cube, crumbled
1 tablespoon light soy sauce

Roughly chop half the chicken. Blend or process chopped chicken, onions, garlic and gingerroot until smooth.

Place 1 level teaspoon of mixture on each pastry sheet, brush edges with blended cornstarch and water.

Gather each pastry sheet to form a pouch around filling, press edges firmly together to seal.

Cut remaining chicken into thin strips, combine in pan with sherry, cook, stirring, 2 minutes or until chicken is tender.

Place extra water in large pan, bring to boil, add chicken mixture, chicken pouches, cabbage, bouillon cube and sauce, simmer, uncovered, 2 minutes.

Serves 6.

- Broth best completed just before serving. Chicken pouches can be made a day ahead.
- Storage: Covered, in refrigerator.
- Freeze: Uncooked pouches suitable.
- Microwave: Not suitable.

LEFT: From top: Chicken Minestrone, Chicken Spinach Chowder with Garlic Croutons.
BELOW: From left: Ginger Chicken Gow Gees in Sherried Broth, Hot and Sour Soup.

MUSHROOM AND CHICKEN SOUP WITH WATERCRESS

1lb chicken breasts
5 cups water
1 onion, chopped
4 cloves
1 teaspoon cuminseed
½ teaspoon dried thyme leaves
8 black peppercorns
½oz Chinese dried mushrooms
2 large potatoes, chopped
6oz button mushrooms, sliced
**1 tablespoon chopped fresh
   watercress**
3 green onions, chopped
1½ tablespoons light soy sauce
1½ tablespoons lemon juice

Combine chicken, water, onion, cloves, cuminseed, thyme and peppercorns in pan. Bring to boil, simmer, covered, about 40 minutes or until chicken is tender. Remove chicken breasts; strain broth into bowl; discard onion mixture. Remove skin from chicken, remove meat from bones, discard skin and bones; chop meat into ½ inch cubes. Skim any fat from broth.

Place dried mushrooms in bowl, cover with boiling water, stand 20 minutes. Drain mushrooms, discard stems, slice mushroom caps finely.

Return reserved broth to pan, add potatoes, bring to boil, simmer, uncovered, until potatoes are soft. Blend or process mixture until smooth, return mixture to pan.

Add chicken meat, all mushrooms, watercress, green onions, sauce and juice to pan, bring to boil, simmer, uncovered, 10 minutes.

Serves 4 to 6.

■ Soup can be made a day ahead.
■ Storage: Covered, in refrigerator.
■ Freeze: Not suitable.
■ Microwave: Suitable.

HERBED CHICKEN, LEEK AND ONION SOUP

1½lb chicken breasts
1½ tablespoons vegetable oil
2 leeks, chopped
2 onions, chopped
2 red onions, chopped
2 carrots, chopped
1 stalk celery, chopped
8 cups water
2 bay leaves
1 tablespoon dried oregano leaves
1 teaspoon fennel seeds
2 zucchini, sliced
5oz yellow pattypan squash, sliced
7 green onions, chopped
¼ cup chopped fresh parsley

Remove skin from chicken, remove meat from bones, reserve bones, discard skin; chop and reserve meat.

Heat oil in large pan, add leeks and onions, cook, stirring, until onions are soft, remove from pan.

Place reserved bones in pan with carrots, celery, water, herbs and seeds. Slowly bring to boil, simmer, partially covered, 1 hour. Strain broth into bowl, reserve broth, discard vegetables and bones. Cool broth, cover, refrigerate several hours or overnight. Skim fat from broth, using slotted spoon.

Just before serving, heat 1½ cups of broth in pan, add reserved chicken meat, bring to boil, simmer, covered, about 3 minutes or until tender; drain and reserve chicken, discard broth.

Combine zucchini, squash, onion mixture and remaining broth in pan. Bring to boil, simmer, covered, 2 minutes. Stir in green onions, parsley and cooked chicken.

Serves 6.

■ Broth can be made 3 days ahead.
■ Storage: Covered, in refrigerator.
■ Freeze: Strained broth suitable.
■ Microwave: Not suitable.

SPICED QUAIL AND POTATO SOUP

3 quail
½ teaspoon coriander seeds
½ teaspoon cuminseed
¼ teaspoon fenugreek seeds
¼ teaspoon black mustard seeds
2 tablespoons (¼ stick) butter
1 onion, chopped
3 cloves garlic, sliced
1 stalk celery, chopped
1 tablespoon all-purpose flour
6 cups water
3 small chicken bouillon
cubes, crumbled
¼ teaspoon turmeric
2 leeks, chopped
2 large old potatoes, chopped
1 small red bell pepper,
finely chopped
6oz frozen broad beans, thawed

Cut drumsticks and wings from quail. Remove breast meat from bones, discard bones and wings. Remove skin from quail pieces; discard skin.

Grind or process seeds until fine. Melt butter in pan, add seeds, cook, stirring, until fragrant. Stir in onion, garlic and celery, cook, stirring, until onion is soft. Stir in flour, stir until lightly browned. Remove from heat, gradually stir in water, bouillon cubes and turmeric. Stir over heat until mixture boils and thickens slightly, simmer, uncovered, 20 minutes.

Just before serving, add leeks and potatoes to pan, bring to boil, simmer, covered, about 10 minutes or until potatoes are tender. Stir in drumsticks and meat, pepper and beans, simmer, covered, about 5 minutes or until meat is just tender.

Serves 4.

- Broth can be prepared a day ahead.
- Storage: Covered, in refrigerator.
- Freeze: Broth suitable.
- Microwave: Not suitable.

CREAMED CORN, HAM AND CHICKEN SOUP

2½lb chicken
1 onion, quartered
6 black peppercorns
4 sprigs fresh parsley
¾in piece gingerroot
8 cups water
2 teaspoons grated gingerroot, extra
1¾ cups canned creamed corn
1½ tablespoons light soy sauce
1 teaspoon Oriental sesame oil
5 green onions, sliced
¼ cup cornstarch
2 egg whites
2½ tablespoons water, extra
5oz cooked ham, finely sliced
2 green onions, chopped, extra

Combine chicken, onion, peppercorns, parsley, gingerroot and water in large pan.

Bring to boil, simmer, covered, 1½ hours. Remove chicken, skim fat from broth, strain broth into bowl, discard onion mixture. Return chicken to broth, cool, cover; refrigerate overnight.

Next day, skim fat from broth, remove chicken from broth. Remove skin from chicken, remove meat from bones, discard skin and bones; chop meat finely.

Combine 6 cups of the broth, extra gingerroot, corn, sauce, oil and green onions in pan, bring to boil. Blend cornstarch and another ¼ cup of the broth, stir into soup, stir until mixture boils and thickens, simmer 1 minute. Discard remaining broth. Beat egg whites and extra water lightly with fork, gradually stir into simmering soup.

Add chicken meat to soup with ham, heat gently. Serve soup sprinkled with extra green onions.

Serves 6.

- Soup best made close to serving.
- Freeze: Not suitable.
- Microwave: Not suitable.

BARBEQUED DUCK SOUP

2½lb Chinese barbequed duck
18 small Chinese dried mushrooms
1 red bell pepper, sliced
1 tablespoon light soy sauce
1 teaspoon oyster-flavored sauce
¼ cup dry sherry
6 green onions, chopped
¾ cup canned sliced bamboo
shoots, drained

CHICKEN BROTH
3lb boiling chicken
2 leeks, sliced
2 carrots, chopped
1 bay leaf
1 teaspoon black peppercorns
10 cups water

Remove meat from duck, leaving skin on. Discard bones, chop meat.

Place mushrooms in bowl, cover with boiling water, stand 20 minutes; drain.

Bring chicken broth to boil, add mushrooms, pepper, sauces, sherry, green onions and bamboo shoots, simmer, uncovered, 10 minutes.

Just before serving, stir in duck meat, cook until heated through.

Chicken Broth: Combine all ingredients in pan; bring to boil, simmer, covered, 3 hours. Strain broth into bowl; reserve chicken for another recipe. Cool broth, cover, refrigerate several hours or overnight. Skim fat from broth.

Serves 6.

- Broth can be made a day ahead. Soup, except for duck meat, can be prepared 6 hours ahead.
- Storage: Covered, in refrigerator.
- Freeze: Broth suitable.
- Microwave: Soup suitable.

LEFT: Clockwise from left: Herbed Chicken, Leek and Onion Soup, Mushroom and Chicken Soup with Watercress, Spiced Quail and Potato Soup.
BELOW: From left: Creamed Corn, Ham and Chicken Soup, Barbequed Duck Soup.

APPETIZERS

The joy of these lovely appetizers is that they are so versatile. Many have dinner-party style; others suit casual entertaining. Some are quite hearty and you could happily serve them as light lunches. Where possible, we have said "makes 6" or "makes 18", etc., instead of the number of serves, so it is even easier to cater for parties. You will find plenty of fresh and imaginative ideas here, using familiar birds plus some you may not have tried before, such as pheasant and quail in exquisite ways.

PEPPERED TURKEY AND CHICKEN TERRINE

1 bunch (1¼lb) spinach

CHICKEN LAYER
1lb ground chicken
1 clove garlic, minced
1 teaspoon chopped fresh thyme
2 teaspoons canned drained green peppercorns
½ cup fresh bread crumbs

TURKEY LAYER
1lb boneless, skinless turkey breast, chopped
1 clove garlic, minced
1 carrot, grated
¼ cup sour cream
1 teaspoon cracked black peppercorns
¼ cup fresh bread crumbs

CREAMY PEPPERCORN SAUCE
1¼ cups half-and-half
2½ tablespoons dry white wine
2½ tablespoons canned drained green peppercorns
1 small chicken bouillon cube, crumbled
2½ tablespoons chopped fresh chives
1 teaspoon cornstarch
1 tablespoon water

Grease 4½ inch x 10 inch ovenproof loaf dish. Add spinach to pan of boiling water, drain immediately, rinse under cold water; drain well. Line base and sides of dish with some of the spinach, allowing leaves to overhang sides of dish.

Spread half the chicken mixture into dish, top with a layer of spinach. Spread turkey mixture over spinach, top with a layer of spinach, then remaining chicken mixture. Place remaining spinach over top, fold in overhanging spinach. Cover dish with greased foil.

Place terrine in roasting pan, pour in enough boiling water to come halfway up sides of loaf dish. Bake in 350°F oven about 1½ hours or until terrine is firm and cooked. Drain away excess liquid, stand terrine 15 minutes before serving sliced with peppercorn sauce.

Chicken Layer: Combine all ingredients in bowl; mix well.

Turkey Layer: Process turkey until ground. Combine with remaining ingredients in bowl; mix well.

Creamy Peppercorn Sauce: Combine half-and-half, wine, peppercorns, bouillon cube and chives in pan. Stir in blended cornstarch and water, stir over heat until mixture boils and thickens.

Serves 8.

- Terrine can be made a day ahead, reheat in water bath.
- Storage: Covered, in refrigerator.
- Freeze: Not suitable.
- Microwave: Not suitable.

CHICKEN TORTELLINI WITH TOMATO MUSHROOM SAUCE

1lb chicken tortellini

TOMATO MUSHROOM SAUCE
1 tablespoon butter
1 small onion, chopped
½lb button mushrooms, sliced
10oz can Tomato Supreme
1 tablespoon tomato paste
½ cup water
1 small chicken bouillon cube, crumbled
2½ tablespoons chopped fresh parsley
1 tablespoon chopped fresh basil
½ teaspoon cracked black peppercorns

Add tortellini to large pan of boiling water, boil, uncovered, until just tender; drain. Serve with tomato mushroom sauce and grated fresh Parmesan cheese, if desired.

Tomato Mushroom Sauce: Heat butter in pan, add onion, cook, stirring, until soft. Add mushrooms to pan, cook, stirring, until soft. Stir in Tomato Supreme, paste, water, bouillon cube, herbs and peppercorns, simmer, uncovered, about 10 minutes or until sauce thickens slightly.

Serves 4.

- Tortellini and sauce can be made a day ahead.
- Storage: Covered, in refrigerator.
- Freeze: Not suitable.
- Microwave: Not suitable.

MINI CHICKEN AND APPLE FLANS

1 tablespoon butter
1 onion, finely chopped
1lb boneless, skinless chicken breasts, finely chopped
1 tablespoon light soy sauce
2½ tablespoons fresh orange juice
½ cup seasoned stuffing mix
2 sheets ready-rolled shortcrust pastry
2 apples, peeled, cored
⅓ cup apple jelly, warmed

Lightly grease 6 shallow, 4 inch flan pans. Heat butter in pan, add onion and chicken, cook, stirring, until chicken is lightly browned. Stir in sauce and juice. Remove from heat, stir in stuffing mix; cool.

Cut 3 rounds from each pastry sheet large enough to line prepared pans; trim edges. Divide chicken mixture between pans. Cut apples into thin wedges, place on chicken mixture; brush with some of the apple jelly.

Just before serving, place pans on baking sheet, bake in 350°F oven about 1 hour or until well browned. Brush flans with remaining jelly before serving.

Makes 6.

- Recipe can be prepared a day ahead.
- Storage: Covered, in refrigerator.
- Freeze: Not suitable.
- Microwave: Not suitable.

LEFT: Clockwise from top left: Mini Chicken and Apple Flan, Peppered Turkey and Chicken Terrine, Chicken Tortellini with Tomato Mushroom Sauce.

FRIED CHICKEN AND SALMON WITH SAFFRON SAUCE

**4 boneless, skinless chicken
   breast halves
4 slices smoked salmon, halved
all-purpose flour
¼ cup vegetable oil**

SAFFRON SAUCE
**2 tablespoons (¼ stick) butter
1 onion, finely chopped
1¼ cups heavy cream
1 teaspoon seeded mustard
¼ teaspoon Worcestershire sauce
5 saffron threads**

Toss chicken and salmon in flour, shake away excess flour. Heat 2 tablespoons of the oil in pan, add chicken, cook until browned all over and tender, remove from pan; keep warm.

Heat remaining oil in same pan, add salmon, cook until lightly browned, remove from pan. Slice chicken thinly, serve with salmon and saffron sauce.

Saffron Sauce: Heat butter in pan, add onion, cook, stirring, until soft. Add cream, mustard, sauce and saffron, bring to boil, simmer, stirring, until saffron sauce thickens slightly.

Serves 4.

■ Recipe best made close to serving.
■ Freeze: Not suitable.
■ Microwave: Sauce suitable.

DEEP-FRIED SHRIMP AND CHICKEN BALLS

**¾ cup basmati rice
2 teaspoons Szechuan pepper
1oz Chinese dried mushrooms
½lb cooked shrimp
1lb ground chicken
2 green onions, finely chopped
1 teaspoon grated gingerroot
1 tablespoon oyster-flavored sauce
½ teaspoon Oriental sesame oil
1 clove garlic, minced
1 egg, lightly beaten
oil for deep-frying**

Stir rice and pepper in heavy-based pan over heat until golden, blend or process until crushed.

Place mushrooms in bowl, cover with boiling water, stand 20 minutes. Drain mushrooms, discard stems, chop caps finely. Shell and devein shrimp, chop shrimp finely.

Combine mushrooms, shrimp, chicken, onions, gingerroot, sauce, sesame oil, garlic and egg in bowl. Shape 1 rounded tablespoon of mixture into a ball, repeat with remaining mixture; toss in rice.

Just before serving, deep-fry balls in hot oil until well browned and cooked through. Serve with mango chutney, if desired.

Makes about 30.

■ Recipe can be prepared a day ahead.
■ Storage: Covered, in refrigerator.
■ Freeze: Not suitable.
■ Microwave: Not suitable.

HONEYED CHICKEN POCKETS WITH CRAB SEASONING

**12 chicken drumsticks
1 tablespoon vegetable oil
1 tablespoon honey**

CRAB SEASONING
**2 tablespoons (¼ stick) butter
1 tablespoon finely chopped
   gingerroot
1 small fresh red chili
   pepper, chopped
1 green onion, chopped
6oz can crab meat, drained
2 teaspoons light soy sauce**

Using sharp knife, cut and scrape meat down bone of each drumstick, working towards the thick end. As you do this, the meat will turn inside out.

Cut across bone, leaving flesh attached to knuckle; discard bone. Turn meat again, so skin is on the outside. Fill pockets with crab seasoning, secure with small skewers or toothpicks.

Just before serving, barbeque or broil drumsticks, brushing frequently with combined oil and honey, until browned and cooked through.

Crab Seasoning: Heat butter in pan, add gingerroot, chili pepper and onion, cook, stirring, until onion is soft. Remove from heat, cool slightly. Stir in flaked crab meat and soy sauce.

Makes 12.

■ Drumsticks can be prepared a
   day ahead.
■ Storage: Covered, in refrigerator.
■ Freeze: Uncooked chicken
   pockets suitable.
■ Microwave: Not suitable.

CREAMY CHICKEN FETTUCCINE

½lb fettuccine pasta
1lb boneless, skinless
    chicken breasts
2 tablespoons (¼ stick) butter
¼ cup (½ stick) butter, extra
1¼ cups heavy cream
1¼ cups (3½ oz) coarsely grated
    fresh Parmesan cheese
1 teaspoon cracked
    black peppercorns
1 clove garlic, minced
2 teaspoons dried basil leaves

Add pasta to large pan of boiling water, boil, uncovered, until just tender, drain; keep warm.

Cut chicken into thin strips. Heat butter in pan, add chicken in batches, cook, stirring, until lightly browned and tender; drain on absorbent paper.

Heat extra butter in pan, add cream, stir until boiling. Add chicken, cheese, peppercorns, garlic and basil, stir until heated through, serve over pasta.

Serves 4.

■ Recipe can be made 2 hours ahead.
■ Storage: Covered, at room
    temperature.
■ Freeze: Not suitable.
■ Microwave: Pasta suitable.

LEFT: Fried Chicken and Salmon with Saffron Sauce.
ABOVE: Clockwise from left: Creamy Chicken Fettuccine, Honeyed Chicken Pockets with Crab Seasoning, Deep-Fried Shrimp and Chicken Balls.

ROCK CORNISH HENS WITH ASPARAGUS AND PROSCIUTTO

4 x ¾lb Rock Cornish hens
1 tablespoon butter, melted
½ teaspoon paprika
2 teaspoons cornstarch
1½ tablespoons sweet chili sauce
¼ cup dry red wine
1 small sprig fresh rosemary
¾ cup water
1 small chicken bouillon cube, crumbled
1 bunch (about ½ lb) fresh
   asparagus, sliced
1½ tablespoons olive oil
3½oz thinly sliced prosciutto
7oz bocconcini, thinly sliced

Cut hens in half, place cut-side-down on wire rack in roasting pan, brush with combined butter and paprika. Bake in 350°F oven about 40 minutes or until well browned and tender; keep warm.

Blend cornstarch with chili sauce and wine in small pan. Stir in rosemary, water and bouillon cube. Stir over heat until mixture boils and thickens slightly; strain.

Boil, steam or microwave asparagus until just tender; drain. Heat oil in pan, add asparagus, prosciutto and cheese, cook, stirring, until heated through. Serve halved hens on asparagus and prosciutto mixture, pour over sauce.

Serves 8.

■ Recipe best made just before serving.
■ Freeze: Not suitable.
■ Microwave: Asparagus and
   sauce suitable.

STIR-FRIED CHICKEN AND NOODLE SALAD

3lb chicken
3½oz Chinese dried noodles
2½ tablespoons vegetable oil
3½oz green beans, chopped
3½oz snow peas
1 carrot, chopped
1 red bell pepper, chopped
1 zucchini, chopped
3½oz bean sprouts
1 orange, segmented
1 tablespoon sliced almonds, toasted
DRESSING
½ stalk celery, finely chopped
6 green onions, chopped
2½ tablespoons light soy sauce
½ cup vegetable oil
½ teaspoon grated gingerroot
1 clove garlic, minced

Place chicken on wire rack in roasting pan, bake, uncovered, in 350°F oven about 1¼ hours or until tender; cool.

Remove skin from chicken, remove meat from bones, discard skin and bones; slice meat.

Add noodles to pan of boiling water, boil, uncovered, until just tender; drain.

Heat oil in wok or pan, add vegetables, stir-fry until just tender; cool. Combine chicken meat, noodles and vegetable mixture in bowl.

Just before serving, add dressing, toss to combine, serve with orange segments and almonds.

Dressing: Combine all ingredients in jar; shake well.

Serves 6.

■ Recipe best made just before serving.
■ Freeze: Not suitable.
■ Microwave: Noodles suitable.

DUCK WITH APPLES AND GINGER SAUCE

4 boneless duck breast halves
1 tablespoon vegetable oil
2 apples
2 tablespoons (¼ stick) butter
¼ cup dark brown sugar
½ cup clear apple juice
1½ teaspoons grated gingerroot
1 cup ginger ale
¼ cup dry sherry
1 teaspoon cornstarch
1 teaspoon water

Trim excess fat from duck. Heat oil in pan, add duck fillets, cook until well browned all over and tender, prick skin during cooking. Remove from heat, keep warm. Drain pan, reserving 1 tablespoon pan juices.

Peel and core apples, cut into thin slices. Add reserved pan juices, butter, sugar, apple juice and gingerroot to pan. Simmer, uncovered, 2 minutes. Add apples, ginger ale and sherry to pan, cook, stirring gently, 3 minutes or until apples are just soft. Remove apples with

slotted spoon. Simmer mixture further 3 minutes or until reduced by half. Stir in blended cornstarch and water. Stir over heat until sauce boils and thickens slightly. Serve duck sliced with apples and ginger sauce.

Serves 4.

■ Recipe best made close to serving.
■ Freeze: Not suitable.
■ Microwave: Not suitable.

LEFT: Rock Cornish Hens with Asparagus and Prosciutto.
ABOVE: From top: Stir-Fried Chicken and Noodle Salad, Duck with Apples and Ginger Sauce.

NUTTY CHICKEN, CHEESE AND PEPPER SALAD

2½ cups (¾lb) chopped
    cooked chicken
2 cups shredded lettuce
1 green onion, chopped
1 small green bell pepper,
    thinly sliced
1 small red bell pepper, thinly sliced
1 bocconcini, thinly sliced
¼ cup pine nuts, toasted
¼ bunch chicory

DRESSING
¼ cup olive oil
¼ cup white vinegar
2 teaspoons chopped fresh parsley
2 teaspoons chopped fresh chives
1 clove garlic, minced

Combine chicken, lettuce, onion, bell peppers, bocconcini and nuts in bowl. Spoon chicken mixture over chicory.
Just before serving, add dressing.
Dressing: Combine all ingredients in jar.

    Serves 4.

■ Can be prepared 6 hours ahead.
■ Storage: Covered, in refrigerator.
■ Freeze: Not suitable.

DUCK AND CHICKEN FLANS

3¾lb duck
1 tablespoon butter
7oz button mushrooms, quartered
1½ tablespoons all-purpose flour
2 chicken thighs, boned,
    skinned, chopped
⅔ cup water
1 tablespoon seeded mustard
1½ tablespoons brandy
½ teaspoon dried thyme leaves

PASTRY
1 cup all-purpose flour
¼ cup (½ stick) butter
¼ teaspoon sugar
¼ cup water
1 egg yolk

TOPPING
4 oz package cream cheese
½ cup sour cream

Lightly grease 8 deep, 3½ inch flan pans. Lightly flour a large oven bag, place duck in bag, secure bag with tie provided. Pierce bag as directed on bag package. Bake in 350°F oven about 1½ hours or until tender; cool. Remove skin from duck, remove meat from bones, discard skin, fat and bones; chop meat finely.

Heat butter in pan, add mushrooms, cook, stirring, until soft. Stir in flour, cook, stirring, 1 minute. Stir in chicken and water, stir until mixture boils and thickens, simmer, 1 minute. Remove from heat, stir in duck, mustard, brandy and thyme; cool.

Divide pastry into 8 portions. Roll each portion on lightly floured surface until large enough to line each prepared pan. Lift pastry into pans, trim edges.

Divide duck mixture between pans, smooth surface. Place pans on baking sheets, bake in 375°F oven 15 minutes. Remove from oven, spread with topping. Bake in 350°F oven about 25 minutes or until lightly browned. Serve hot.
Pastry: Process flour, butter and sugar until combined. Add water and egg yolk, process until mixture forms a ball. Turn dough onto floured surface, knead until smooth, cover, refrigerate 30 minutes.
Topping: Beat cheese and cream in small bowl with electric mixer.

    Makes 8.

■ Flans can be made a day ahead.
■ Storage: Covered, in refrigerator.
■ Freeze: Pastry suitable.
■ Microwave: Not suitable.

PEACHY DUCK ROLLS

4 boneless duck breast halves
¾lb ground pork and veal
2 teaspoons brown vinegar
1 tablespoon dark brown sugar
¼ cup heavy cream
½ teaspoon allspice
pinch cayenne pepper
1 teaspoon white mustard seeds
1 tablespoon chopped fresh chives

PEACH SAUCE
29oz can peach halves in light syrup
2 teaspoons chopped fresh mint
¼ cup marmalade
2 teaspoons cornstarch
1 tablespoon water

Pound duck fillets between sheets of plastic wrap until ¼ inch thick. Process pork and veal, vinegar, sugar, cream, allspice and cayenne until smooth. Transfer mixture to bowl, stir in seeds and chives. Spoon mixture along center of each duck fillet. Roll fillets to enclose filling, secure with toothpicks or skewers.

Place rolls on wire rack in roasting pan, bake in 350°F oven about 1 hour or until well browned and cooked through. Pierce skin all over after 30 minutes cooking time. Stand 5 minutes before slicing, serve hot with peach sauce and sliced reserved peaches.
Peach Sauce: Reserve 4 peach halves for serving. Blend remaining peaches with their liquid, mint and marmalade until well combined. Transfer to small pan, stir in blended cornstarch and water, stir until sauce boils and thickens, simmer 1 minute. Remove from heat, strain.

    Serves 8.

■ Recipe can be made 6 hours ahead.
■ Storage: Covered, in refrigerator.
■ Freeze: Uncooked rolls suitable.
■ Microwave: Sauce suitable.

LEFT: Clockwise from top: Nutty Chicken, Cheese and Pepper Salad, Peachy Duck Rolls, Duck and Chicken Flan.

Return wing to normal shape ready for filling with carrot and ham mixture.

Combine sesame oil, hoisin sauce, gingerroot, seeds, ham, carrot and pepper in bowl. Spoon filling into wings, secure openings with toothpicks or skewers. Brush with combined soy sauce, spice powder and honey.

Just before serving, deep-fry wings in hot oil until well browned and cooked through; drain on absorbent paper. Serve wings brushed with combined vinegar, extra hoisin sauce and extra honey.

Makes 12.

■ Recipe can be prepared several hours ahead.
■ Storage: Covered, in refrigerator.
■ Freeze: Uncooked wings suitable.
■ Microwave: Not suitable.

FRIED CHICKEN KABOBS WITH CHILI GARLIC SAUCE

1¼lb chicken thighs, boned, skinned
1 teaspoon grated gingerroot
2½ tablespoons light soy sauce
1 tablespoon dry sherry
cornstarch
oil for shallow-frying

CHILI GARLIC SAUCE
½ cup light soy sauce
⅓ cup dry sherry
1 small fresh red chili pepper, finely chopped
2 cloves garlic, sliced

Cut chicken into 1 inch pieces. Press gingerroot between 2 spoons to extract juice; discard pulp. Combine chicken, gingerroot juice, sauce and sherry in bowl, cover; refrigerate 30 minutes.

Just before serving, thread chicken onto 24 small skewers, toss kabobs in cornstarch, shake away excess cornstarch. Shallow-fry kabobs in hot oil until well browned and tender; drain on absorbent paper. Serve kabobs with chili garlic sauce for dipping.

Chili Garlic Sauce: Combine all ingredients in bowl, cover; stand 30 minutes before using.

Makes 24.

■ Recipe can be prepared a day ahead.
■ Storage: Covered, in refrigerator.
■ Freeze: Uncooked kabobs suitable.
■ Microwave: Not suitable.

CHICKEN MOUSSELINES WITH ORANGE HOLLANDAISE

¾lb boneless, skinless chicken breasts, chopped
2 egg whites
5oz ricotta cheese
½ teaspoon grated orange zest
½ cup heavy cream
2½ tablespoons chopped chives

ORANGE HOLLANDAISE
2½ tablespoons fresh orange juice
2½ tablespoons white vinegar
4 cardamom pods, crushed
2 egg yolks
½ cup (1 stick) butter, melted

Lightly grease 6 timbale molds (½ cup capacity). Process chicken, egg whites, cheese and zest until smooth. Add cream, process until just combined. Stir in chives, cover; refrigerate 30 minutes.

Spoon mixture evenly into prepared molds, place into roasting pan with enough hot water to come halfway up sides of molds. Cover dish with foil. Bake in 325°F oven about 45 minutes or until firm. Stand 5 minutes before turning onto serving plates. Serve mousselines with orange hollandaise.

Orange Hollandaise: Combine juice, vinegar and cardamom in pan, bring to boil, simmer, uncovered, until reduced by half. Strain, reserve liquid, discard pods.

Blend or process egg yolks and reserved liquid until smooth. Gradually pour in hot bubbling butter while motor is operating, blend until thick and smooth.

Serves 6.

■ Recipe best made close to serving.
■ Freeze: Not suitable.
■ Microwave: Not suitable.

SWEET AND SOUR WINGS WITH CARROT HAM FILLING

12 (about 2lb) chicken wings
½ teaspoon Oriental sesame oil
1 tablespoon hoisin sauce
1 teaspoon grated gingerroot
1 teaspoon sesame seeds
2 slices cooked ham, finely chopped
1 cup (¼lb) coarsely grated carrot
1 small red bell pepper, finely chopped
2½ tablespoons light soy sauce
¼ teaspoon five-spice powder
1 teaspoon honey
oil for deep-frying
1½ tablespoons white vinegar
1 tablespoon hoisin sauce, extra
1 tablespoon honey, extra

Cut tip from each wing; discard tips. Without cutting through skin, cut flesh away from bones by scraping down to the first joint. Pull flesh back over joint, cut flesh away from joint. Push and scrape flesh to end of wing, remove bones.

ABOVE: Clockwise from left: wing tips removed, boned wings, bones removed, scraping meat from bones.

ABOVE: Chicken Mousseline with Orange Hollandaise.
RIGHT: From top: Fried Chicken Kabobs with Chili Garlic Sauce, Sweet and Sour Wings with Carrot Ham Filling.

BRANDIED CHICKEN LIVER PATE

¼ cup (½ stick) butter
2 onions, chopped
2 cloves garlic, minced
1lb chicken livers
3 hard-boiled eggs, chopped
¼ teaspoon ground nutmeg
½ teaspoon mixed spice
¼ cup brandy
1 cup (2 sticks) butter, melted, extra

Heat butter in pan, add onions and garlic, cook, stirring, until onions are soft. Add livers, cook, stirring, about 3 minutes or until livers are browned.

Blend or process liver mixture, eggs and spices until finely chopped. With motor operating, pour in brandy and extra butter, process until smooth.

Pour mixture into 8 dishes (½ cup capacity); cover, refrigerate until firm.

Serve pate with toast and crisp vegetable sticks, if desired.

Serves 8.

■ Pate can be made 2 days ahead.
■ Storage: Covered, in refrigerator.
■ Freeze: Not suitable.
■ Microwave: Suitable.

PHEASANT WITH APRICOT COCONUT SEASONING

2lb pheasant
¼ cup honey
1 cup fresh orange juice
¼ cup dry sherry
¼ cup vegetable oil
2 teaspoons cornstarch
2½ tablespoons water

APRICOT COCONUT SEASONING
¼ cup (½ stick) butter
1 onion, finely chopped
1 green onion, chopped
¼ cup chopped dried apricots
½ cup coconut
½ cup fresh bread crumbs

Remove leg and thigh portions from pheasant. Cut through thigh to leg joint, remove thigh bone.

Boned thigh portions are shown at back of picture. Next, remove and discard wing tips. Remove wing and breast portions; flatten breasts slightly using meat mallet.

Divide apricot coconut seasoning between pheasant portions, fold portions around seasoning, secure with small skewers or toothpicks.

Combine honey, juice, sherry and oil in large bowl, add pheasant; mix until pheasant is coated with honey mixture. Cover, refrigerate pheasant several hours or overnight.

Just before serving, drain pheasant; reserve marinade. Place pheasant portions on wire rack in roasting pan. Bake in 350°F oven about 35 minutes or until well browned and cooked through.

Place reserved marinade in small pan, bring to boil. Stir in blended cornstarch and water, stir until mixture boils and thickens slightly; strain. Remove skewers from pheasant, serve sliced with sauce.

Apricot Coconut Seasoning: Heat butter in pan, add onion, cook, stirring, until soft. Remove from heat, stir in chopped onion, chopped apricots, coconut and bread crumbs.

Serves 4.

- Recipe can be prepared 2 days ahead.
- Storage: Covered, in refrigerator.
- Freeze: Uncooked, seasoned pheasant suitable.
- Microwave: Sauce suitable.

QUAIL AND BEAN SALAD WITH PASSION FRUIT DRESSING

4 quail
¼ cup dry red wine
3 cloves garlic, minced
10oz can three bean mix, rinsed, drained
¾ cup canned sliced water chestnuts, drained
1 red bell pepper, chopped
1 zucchini, thinly sliced
2½ tablespoons olive oil
lettuce

PASSION FRUIT DRESSING
2½ tablespoons olive oil
2½ tablespoons passion fruit pulp
1 tablespoon lemon juice
1 tablespoon chopped fresh parsley

Bone quail following instructions in "Pre-Cooking Preparations" at the back of this book. Halve quail, remove wings and legs. Combine quail pieces, wine and garlic in bowl; cover, refrigerate 2 hours, turning occasionally.

Combine beans, chestnuts, pepper and zucchini in bowl. Add passion fruit dressing, toss, refrigerate 2 hours.

Drain quail pieces, discard liquid. Heat oil in pan, add quail pieces, cook until quail pieces are browned all over and cooked through, drain on absorbent paper; cool.

Stir quail wings and legs into bean mixture. Cut remaining quail into strips, add to salad. Serve with lettuce.

Passion Fruit Dressing: Combine all ingredients in jar: shake well.

Serves 4.

- Recipe can be prepared a day ahead.
- Storage: Covered, in refrigerator.
- Freeze: Not suitable.
- Microwave: Not suitable.

LEFT: Clockwise from top left: Quail and Bean Salad with Passion Fruit Dressing, Pheasant with Apricot Coconut Seasoning, Brandied Chicken Liver Pate.

LEMONY QUAIL WITH VEAL AND PISTACHIO SEASONING

6 quail
1½oz chicken livers, chopped
3 green onions, chopped
½lb ground veal
1 tablespoon chopped pistachios
1 teaspoon light soy sauce
¼ teaspoon grated gingerroot
1½ teaspoons grated lemon zest
1 tablespoon lemon juice
1 tablespoon chopped fresh parsley
2½ tablespoons vegetable oil

LEMON SAUCE
1 cup water
1 small chicken bouillon
  cube, crumbled
½ cup half-and-half
1 tablespoon lemon juice
2 teaspoons cornstarch
2 teaspoons water, extra
1 tablespoon chopped fresh parsley

Bone quail following instructions in "Pre-Cooking Preparations" at the back of this book; leave wings and legs intact.

Combine livers, onions, veal, nuts, sauce, gingerroot, zest, juice and parsley in bowl; mix well. Place quail skin-side-down onto bench, top with veal mixture. Fold in sides of quail to overlap, secure with small skewers or toothpicks; tie quail legs together.

Just before serving, heat oil in pan, add quail, cook until lightly browned all over. Transfer quail to roasting pan, bake in 375°F oven about 20 minutes or until well browned and tender. Stand quail 5 minutes, remove skewers, untie legs. Serve with lemon sauce.

Lemon Sauce: Combine water, bouillon cube, half-and-half, juice, blended cornstarch and extra water in pan. Stir over heat until mixture boils and thickens slightly, stir in parsley.

Serves 6.

- Recipe can be prepared a day ahead.
- Storage: Covered, in refrigerator.
- Freeze: Uncooked seasoned quail suitable.
- Microwave: Sauce suitable.

ROCK CORNISH HENS WITH ORANGE LIQUEUR SAUCE

3 x 1lb Rock Cornish hens
¼ cup (½ stick) butter, melted
1 clove garlic, minced

ORANGE LIQUEUR SAUCE
1 tablespoon vegetable oil
2 tablespoons (¼ stick) butter
2 onions, sliced
2½ tablespoons Grand Marnier
¼ cup dry white wine
2 cups fresh orange juice
1½oz package French onion
  soup mix
¼ cup finely shredded orange zest
½ teaspoon dried tarragon leaves

Cut hens in half, place cut-side-down on wire rack in roasting pan, brush with combined butter and garlic. Bake in 350°F oven about 30 minutes or until lightly browned. Pour orange liqueur sauce over hens, cover, bake in 350°F oven about 15 minutes or until hens are tender.

Orange Liqueur Sauce: Heat oil and butter in pan, add onions, cook, stirring, until soft. Stir in liqueur, wine and half the juice. Bring to boil, simmer, uncovered, until reduced by half. Stir in remaining juice, dry soup mix, zest and tarragon, simmer 1 minute.

Serves 6.

- Best prepared just before serving. Sauce can be made 3 hours ahead.
- Storage: Covered, in refrigerator.
- Freeze: Not suitable.
- Microwave: Not suitable.

CRISP CHICKEN PUFFS WITH LEMON SAUCE

½lb ground chicken
2 green onions, chopped
1 clove garlic, minced
½ teaspoon grated gingerroot
1 teaspoon light soy sauce
1 teaspoon dry sherry
¼ teaspoon Oriental sesame oil
3 sheets ready-rolled puff pastry
1 egg, lightly beaten
oil for deep-frying

LEMON SAUCE
½ cup lemon juice
¼ cup granulated sugar
2 teaspoons dry sherry
1 teaspoon light soy sauce
1½ tablespoons cornstarch
½ cup water

Combine chicken, onions, garlic, gingerroot, sauce, sherry and sesame oil in bowl. Cut 27 x 3 inch rounds from pastry. Top each round with 1½ level teaspoons of chicken mixture, brush edges lightly with egg, fold in half to enclose filling. Roll and fold edges over to seal.

Just before serving, deep-fry puffs in hot oil until lightly browned and cooked through; drain on absorbent paper. Serve with lemon sauce.

Lemon Sauce: Combine juice, sugar, sherry and sauce in pan. Stir in blended cornstarch and water, stir over heat until mixture boils and thickens.

Makes 27.

- Sauce and puffs can be prepared separately 2 days ahead.
- Storage: Covered, in refrigerator.
- Freeze: Uncooked puffs suitable.
- Microwave: Sauce suitable.

LEFT: From top: Lemony Quail with Veal and Pistachio Seasoning, Rock Cornish Hens with Orange Liqueur Sauce.
BELOW: Crisp Chicken Puffs with Lemon Sauce.

20 minutes or until lightly browned and tender. Remove skewers, cut quail in half, serve with rice and pepper mixture and sherry sauce.

Sherry Sauce: Combine water, sherry and bouillon cubes in pan, bring to boil. Stir in blended cornstarch and extra water, stir until sauce boils and thickens slightly.

Serves 2 to 4.

- Recipe can be prepared a day ahead.
- Storage: Covered, in refrigerator.
- Freeze: Not suitable.
- Microwave: Rice and sauce suitable.

BROILED QUAIL WITH EGGPLANT SALAD

2 teaspoons cracked coriander seeds
2½ tablespoons olive oil
⅓ cup lemon juice
2 teaspoons dried oregano leaves
½ teaspoon dried thyme leaves
2 cloves garlic, minced
1 teaspoon light soy sauce
4 quail, halved

EGGPLANT SALAD
1 large eggplant
2 large tomatoes
salt
¼ cup olive oil
24 black olives
3 oz feta cheese, finely chopped

Combine seeds, oil, juice, herbs, garlic and sauce in jug. Pour half the marinade over quail in bowl; cover, refrigerate several hours or overnight. Reserve remaining marinade for eggplant salad.

Drain quail, reserve marinade. Broil quail, brushing with this reserved marinade, until well browned and cooked through. Serve quail with eggplant salad.

Eggplant Salad: Cut eggplant and tomatoes into thin slices. Place eggplant slices on wire rack, sprinkle with salt, stand 20 minutes. Rinse eggplant, drain on absorbent paper. Heat oil in pan, add eggplant slices in batches, cook until lightly browned and soft.

Combine eggplant, tomatoes, olives, cheese and reserved marinade in bowl.

Serves 8.

- Quail best cooked just before serving. Salad can be made 6 hours ahead.
- Storage: Salad, covered, in refrigerator.
- Freeze: Not suitable.
- Microwave: Not suitable.

QUAIL WITH MUSHROOMS, PROSCIUTTO AND WILD RICE

2 quail
1 tablespoon butter
1 small onion, chopped
3oz mushrooms, finely chopped
2½ tablespoons dry white wine
⅓ cup packaged bread crumbs
1 teaspoon chopped fresh basil
2 slices prosciutto
5oz wild rice
1 red bell pepper, finely sliced
1 tablespoon vegetable oil

SHERRY SAUCE
1 cup water
⅓ cup sweet sherry
2 small chicken bouillon cubes, crumbled
1 tablespoon cornstarch
¼ cup water, extra

Bone quail following instructions in "Pre-Cooking Preparations" at the back of this book; leave legs and wings intact.

Heat butter in pan, add onion, cook, stirring, until soft. Add mushrooms and wine, bring to boil, simmer, uncovered, stirring occasionally, until most of the liquid is evaporated. Remove from heat, stir in bread crumbs and basil; cool.

Place quail skin-side-down on bench, top with mushroom mixture. Fold in sides of quail to overlap, secure with small skewers or toothpicks; tie legs together. Wrap a piece of prosciutto around each quail, secure with toothpicks.

Just before serving, add rice to large pan of boiling water, boil, uncovered, about 30 minutes or until tender; drain. Combine rice with pepper; keep warm.

Place quail on wire rack in roasting pan, brush with oil. Bake in 350°F oven about

ABOVE: Quail with Mushrooms, Prosciutto and Wild Rice.
RIGHT: Broiled Quail with Eggplant Salad.

SPECIAL OCCASIONS

For gala days and dinners we've devised flavorful dishes that create a sense of occasion but are not too difficult to make. For the grandest entrance you could choose a beautifully browned and glistening turkey, duck or goose with lovely seasoning and sauce (the turkey is lavished with rich cashew seasoning and mango sauce, for example). Rock Cornish hens, quail, pheasant and, of course, chicken come to the party in fine style, too. Then there's the delight of the new, such as crumbed, fried duck sausage with pepper pasta and ballotines with lentil chili sauce; even quickly cooked fillets are transformed into wonderful meals with superb sauces of many kinds.

ROCK CORNISH HENS WITH PEPPER AND BASIL SEASONING

6 x ¾lb Rock Cornish hens
¼ cup (½ stick) butter, melted
2½ tablespoons lemon juice
1 tablespoon honey
2½ tablespoons light soy sauce

PEPPER AND BASIL SEASONING
¼ cup (½ stick) butter
¼ cup chopped fresh chives
1 clove garlic, minced
¼ cup pine nuts
1½ cups (3½oz) fresh bread crumbs
1 teaspoon grated lemon zest
2 red bell peppers, chopped
¼ cup chopped fresh basil

Cut hens in half through backbone, leaving breastbone intact. Place each hen on hard surface with breast facing upwards. Press down firmly on breast with palm of hand to flatten.

Loosen skin by sliding fingers between skin and meat. Gently push seasoning evenly under skin. Tuck wings under bodies. Place hens cut-side-down in single layer in roasting pan, brush with combined butter and juice. Bake in 350°F oven about 40 minutes or until browned and tender. Brush hens with combined honey and sauce, bake further 5 minutes. Cut completely in half before serving.
Pepper and Basil Seasoning: Melt butter in pan, add chives and garlic, cook, stirring, 1 minute. Stir in nuts, bread crumbs, zest, peppers and basil; cook, stirring, 2 minutes.

Serves 6.

- Recipe can be prepared a day ahead.
- Storage: Covered, in refrigerator.
- Freeze: Uncooked seasoned hens suitable.
- Microwave: Not suitable.

ROCK CORNISH HENS WITH BACON AND SAGE SAUCE

4 x 1lb Rock Cornish hens
1 tablespoon butter, melted

BACON AND SAGE SAUCE
1½ tablespoons vegetable oil
2 red onions, chopped
3 cloves garlic, minced
½lb slices bacon, chopped
1 cup water
1 small chicken bouillon cube, crumbled
⅓ cup dry white wine
2 teaspoons seeded mustard
⅓ cup heavy cream
2½ tablespoons chopped fresh sage

Tie legs together, tuck wings under. Place hens on wire rack in roasting pan, brush with butter. Bake in 350°F oven about 45 minutes or until browned and tender. Serve hens with bacon and sage sauce.
Bacon and Sage Sauce: Heat oil in pan, add onions, garlic and bacon, cook, stirring, until onion is soft and bacon lightly browned. Add water, bouillon cube, wine and mustard. Bring to boil, simmer, uncovered, about 5 minutes or until reduced to about 1 cup. Stir in cream and sage, stir until heated through.

Serves 4.

- Sauce can be made a day ahead.
- Storage: Covered, in refrigerator.
- Freeze: Not suitable.
- Microwave: Not suitable.

CHICKEN WITH FIG AND PORT SAUCE

4 boneless, skinless chicken breast halves
all-purpose flour
2 tablespoons (¼ stick) butter
1 tablespoon port wine
½ cup water
½ cup dry white wine
1 small chicken bouillon cube, crumbled
3 dried figs, sliced
2½ tablespoons heavy cream

Toss chicken in flour, shake away excess flour. Heat butter in pan, add chicken in single layer, cook until well browned all over. Add port, water, wine, bouillon cube and figs to pan. Bring to boil, simmer, covered, about 10 minutes or until chicken is tender. Remove chicken from

pan, bring sauce to boil, boil rapidly, uncovered, 2 minutes. Remove from heat, stir in cream. Serve chicken with fig and port sauce.

Serves 4.

■ Recipe best made just before serving.
■ Freeze: Not suitable.
■ Microwave: Not suitable.

ABOVE: Clockwise from top: Rock Cornish Hen with Bacon and Sage Sauce, Chicken with Fig and Port Sauce, Rock Cornish Hens with Pepper and Basil Seasoning.

PAN-FRIED CHICKEN WITH CREAMY PORT SAUCE

**8 boneless, skinless chicken
   breast halves**
all-purpose flour
2 tablespoons (¼ stick) butter

CREAMY PORT SAUCE
1 cup water
⅔ cup dry white wine
½ cup port wine
**1 small chicken bouillon
   cube, crumbled**
⅓ cup heavy cream

Toss chicken in flour, shake away excess flour. Heat butter in pan, add chicken, cook until well browned all over and tender. Remove chicken from pan; keep warm. Drain excess fat from pan, use pan for sauce.

Creamy Port Sauce: Add water, wine, port and bouillon cube to pan, bring to boil, simmer, uncovered, about 5 minutes or until reduced by half. Remove from heat, stir in cream.

   Serves 4 to 8.

■ Best made just before serving.
■ Freeze: Not suitable.
■ Microwave: Not suitable.

ABOVE: Clockwise from top: Pot Roast Pheasants, Spiced Quail with Curried Butter Sauce, Pan-Fried Chicken with Creamy Port Sauce.
ABOVE RIGHT: Rock Cornish Hen with Sun-Dried Tomato Tapenade.

SPICED QUAIL WITH CURRIED BUTTER SAUCE

6 quail
½ teaspoon grated gingerroot
½ teaspoon ground cardamom
½ teaspoon ground cumin
1½ tablespoons lime juice
1 tablespoon olive oil
½lb green beans, chopped
½ x 19oz can white kidney beans
    (cannellini), rinsed, drained
1 tablespoon chopped fresh chives

CURRIED BUTTER SAUCE
2 egg yolks
2 teaspoons curry powder
1 tablespoon lemon juice
1 clove garlic, minced
1 teaspoon dry mustard
½ cup (1 stick) butter, melted

Combine quail, gingerroot, cardamom, cumin and juice in bowl, cover; refrigerate several hours or overnight.

Just before serving, tie legs together, cover legs with foil. Place quail on wire rack in roasting pan, bake in 350˚F oven about 30 minutes or until well browned and tender. Remove from oven; cover with foil, keep quail warm.

Heat oil in pan, add green beans, cook, stirring, 5 minutes, stir in kidney beans and chives. Serve quail over beans, topped with curried butter sauce.

Curried Butter Sauce: Blend or process egg yolks, curry powder, juice, garlic and mustard until smooth. With motor operating, pour in hot bubbling butter a little at a time, blend until mixture is thickened.

Serves 6.

- Quail can be prepared 2 days ahead.
- Storage: Covered, in refrigerator.
- Freeze: Marinated quail suitable.
- Microwave: Not suitable.

POT ROAST PHEASANTS

2 x 1½lb pheasants
2½ tablespoons olive oil
2 large onions, thinly sliced
2 large carrots, sliced diagonally
2½ tablespoons olive oil, extra
6oz slices bacon, chopped
2 sprigs fresh rosemary
2 bay leaves
¼ cup dry white wine
½ cup water
⅓ cup redcurrant jelly, warmed
1 tablespoon balsamic vinegar
1 tablespoon all-purpose flour
¼ cup water, extra

Remove and discard head and feet from pheasants. Rinse pheasants under cold water, pat dry with absorbent paper. Cut each pheasant into 4 portions.

Heat oil in large pan, add onions and carrots, cook, stirring, until onions are soft. Drain on absorbent paper.

Heat extra oil in same pan, add pheasant in batches, cook until well

browned all over; drain on absorbent paper. Add bacon to pan, cook, stirring, 2 minutes. Return onion mixture and pheasant to pan, stir in herbs, wine, water, jelly and vinegar. Bring to boil, simmer, covered, about 1 hour or until pheasant is cooked through.

Remove pheasant from pan, stir in blended flour and extra water to pan, stir until sauce boils and thickens. Return pheasant to pan to reheat.

Serves 4.

- Recipe can be made a day ahead.
- Storage: Covered, in refrigerator.
- Freeze: Suitable.
- Microwave: Not suitable.

ROCK CORNISH HENS WITH SUN-DRIED TOMATO TAPENADE

3 green onions, chopped
⅓ cup dry white wine
⅓ cup sake
½ cup light soy sauce
4 x 1lb Rock Cornish hens
¼ cup honey
oil for deep-frying

SUN-DRIED TOMATO TAPENADE
½ cup drained sun-dried tomatoes
⅔ cup pitted black olives
1 clove garlic, minced
2 teaspoons fresh thyme leaves
¼ cup olive oil

Blend or process onions and wine until smooth, add sake and sauce, blend until combined. Pour mixture over hens in shallow dish, cover, refrigerate several hours or overnight.

Add hens separately to large pan of boiling water for 1 minute, drain. Cut each hen in half lengthways. Place cut-side-down on tray, brush hens with honey, stand 15 minutes.

Just before serving, deep-fry each half in hot oil, turning occasionally to prevent skin from over-browning, until cooked through; drain on absorbent paper. Serve with sun-dried tomato tapenade.

Sun-Dried Tomato Tapenade: Blend or process tomatoes, olives, garlic and thyme until smooth. While motor is operating, add oil gradually in a thin stream.

Serves 4 to 8.

- Hens can be prepared a day ahead. Tapenade can be made a week ahead.
- Storage: Covered, in refrigerator.
- Freeze: Not suitable.
- Microwave: Not suitable.

SPICY ROAST GOOSE WITH BAKED ONIONS

1 tablespoon vegetable oil
2 teaspoons ground cumin
2 teaspoons curry powder
1 teaspoon ground coriander
2 cloves garlic, minced
7lb goose
all-purpose flour
6 onions, quartered

Combine oil, spices, coriander and garlic in bowl, rub mixture over goose. Tie legs together, tuck wings under. Prick skin all over to release fat in cooking, but not through to the flesh.

Lightly flour a large oven bag, place goose and onions in bag, secure with tie provided. Make holes in bag as advised on package. Place goose breast-side-up in roasting pan, bake in 375˚F oven about 2 hours or until goose is tender. Serve goose with onions.

Serves 6 to 8.

■ Recipe best made close to serving.
■ Freeze: Not suitable.
■ Microwave: Not suitable.

GOOSE WITH FRUIT AND NUT SEASONING

1 tablespoon butter, melted
1 tablespoon honey
1 teaspoon light soy sauce
7lb goose
all-purpose flour
FRUIT AND NUT SEASONING
2½ tablespoons vegetable oil
½lb chicken giblets, finely chopped
1 onion, finely chopped
1 stalk celery, chopped
1 apple, peeled, chopped
½ cup chopped Brazil nuts
½ cup slivered almonds
½ cup thinly sliced dried apricots
½ cup finely chopped dark seedless raisins
1 tablespoon chopped fresh mint
1½ cups (3½oz) fresh bread crumbs

Combine butter, honey and sauce in bowl, brush mixture over inside and outside of goose. Fill goose with fruit and nut seasoning, secure opening with skewers. Tie legs together, tuck wings under. Prick skin all over to release fat in cooking, but not through to the goose flesh.

Lightly flour a large oven bag, place goose in bag, secure with tie provided. Make holes in bag as advised on package. Place goose breast-side-up in roasting pan, bake in 375˚F oven about 2 hours or until tender.

Fruit and Nut Seasoning: Heat half the oil in pan, add giblets, cook, stirring, until browned, remove from pan; drain. Add remaining oil to pan, add onion and celery, cook, stirring, until onion is soft. Add apple and nuts, cook, stirring, until nuts are lightly browned. Remove from heat, stir in giblets, apricots and raisins, mint and bread crumbs; cool.

Serves 6 to 8.

■ Recipe can be prepared a day ahead.
■ Storage: Covered, in refrigerator.
■ Freeze: Uncooked seasoned goose suitable.
■ Microwave: Not suitable.

CRUMBED ROCK CORNISH HENS WITH HERBED CREAM

3 x 1lb Rock Cornish hens, halved
all-purpose flour
2 eggs, lightly beaten
2 cups (5oz) fresh bread crumbs
oil for deep-frying
6 x ¾ inch slices dense
    whole-wheat bread
3oz (¾ stick) butter
2 teaspoons dried mixed herbs

HERBED CREAM
1¼ cups heavy cream
2 teaspoons French mustard
2 teaspoons chopped fresh parsley
2 teaspoons chopped fresh basil
1 teaspoon chopped fresh mint
1 tablespoon brandy

Toss hen halves in flour, shake away excess flour. Dip in eggs, then in bread crumbs to coat. Place on tray, cover, refrigerate 20 minutes.

Deep-fry hen halves in batches in hot oil until lightly browned but not cooked through. Place cut-side-down on rack in roasting pan, bake in 350°F oven about 25 minutes or until tender.

Spread 1 side of each bread slice with butter, sprinkle with herbs. Place bread on baking sheet, bake in 350°F oven about 20 minutes or until browned and crisp. Serve hen halves on bread, topped with herbed cream.

Herbed Cream: Combine all ingredients in pan, stir over heat until mixture boils, simmer, stirring occasionally, about 10 minutes or until slightly thickened.

Serves 6.

- ■ Recipe best made just before serving.
- ■ Freeze: Not suitable.
- ■ Microwave: Not suitable.

DUCK MARYLANDS WITH ORANGE SAUCE

3oz (¾ stick) butter
1 tablespoon vegetable oil
1 tablespoon grated orange zest
1½ tablespoons superfine sugar
4 duck marylands (thighs with legs)

ORANGE SAUCE
1 tablespoon white vinegar
1½ tablespoons superfine sugar
2½ tablespoons brandy
2 teaspoons grated orange zest
1 cup fresh orange juice
1 tablespoon cornstarch

Heat butter and oil in pan, add zest and sugar, cook, stirring, until sugar is dissolved. Add marylands, cook until lightly browned all over, transfer to ovenproof dish, reserve ¼ cup pan juices for sauce.

Bake marylands, covered, in 350°F oven 30 minutes, uncover, bake marylands further 30 minutes or until well browned and tender. Serve marylands with orange sauce.

Orange Sauce: Heat reserved pan juices in pan. Add vinegar, sugar, brandy, zest and ¾ cup of the juice, stir over heat without boiling until sugar is dissolved. Stir in blended cornstarch and remaining juice, stir until sauce boils and thickens.

Serves 4.

- ■ Recipe best made just before serving.
- ■ Freeze: Not suitable.
- ■ Microwave: Sauce suitable.

LEFT: From left: Spicy Roast Goose with Baked Onions, Goose with Fruit and Nut Seasoning.
ABOVE: From top: Duck Maryland with Orange Sauce, Crumbed Rock Cornish Hen with Herbed Cream.

QUAIL WITH ALMOND RICE SEASONING AND GRAPES

4 quail
1 tablespoon butter, melted

ALMOND RICE SEASONING
¾ cup cooked rice
1 teaspoon chopped fresh rosemary
2 teaspoons French mustard
2 teaspoons honey
**2½ tablespoons chopped
     fresh parsley**
¼ cup sliced almonds, toasted

GRAPE SAUCE
1 tablespoon butter
1 green onion, chopped
1½ tablespoons all-purpose flour
1 cup dark grape juice
2½ tablespoons port wine
2½ tablespoons water
1 teaspoon Worcestershire sauce
¼lb dark grapes

Tuck wings under bodies, fill quail with almond rice seasoning. Cut a small hole on each side of skin flap near cavity openings. Push legs diagonally through opposite holes to hold legs securely.

Place quail on wire rack in roasting pan, brush with butter. Bake in 350°F oven about 30 minutes or until well browned and tender. Serve quail halved with grape sauce.

Almond Rice Seasoning: Combine all ingredients in bowl; mix well.

Grape Sauce: Melt butter in pan, add onion, cook, stirring, until soft. Stir in flour, cook, stirring, until flour is lightly browned. Remove from heat, gradually stir in combined juice, port, water and sauce. Stir over heat until sauce boils and thickens, strain; add grapes.

Serves 4.

■ Quail can be prepared a day ahead.
■ Storage: Covered, in refrigerator.
■ Freeze: Uncooked quail suitable.
■ Microwave: Not suitable.

GINGER WINE DUCK WITH ORANGE DUMPLINGS

6 boneless duck breast halves
1 cup port wine
1 teaspoon grated orange zest
1 cup fresh orange juice
⅔ cup green ginger wine

ORANGE DUMPLINGS
1 cup self-rising flour
2 green onions, chopped
1 teaspoon superfine sugar
½ teaspoon grated orange zest
1½ tablespoons butter, melted
2½ tablespoons milk
**¼ cup fresh orange
     juice, approximately**
**2 small chicken bouillon
     cubes, crumbled**
2 cups water

Combine duck, port, zest, juice and ginger wine in bowl, cover, refrigerate overnight.

Just before serving, drain duck, reserve marinade; prick skin well. Place duck fillets in single layer on wire rack in roasting pan, bake, uncovered, in 350°F oven about 30 minutes or until well browned and tender. Heat reserved marinade in pan until boiling, simmer, uncovered, until reduced by about half. Serve with duck fillets and orange dumplings.

Orange Dumplings: Sift flour into bowl, stir in onions, sugar and zest. Stir in butter, milk and enough juice to form a soft dough. Roll rounded tablespoons of dough into balls.

Heat bouillon cubes and water in pan until simmering. Add dumplings, simmer, uncovered, until doubled in size and cooked through; drain dumplings on absorbent paper.

Serves 6.

■ Recipe can be prepared a day ahead.
■ Storage: Covered, in refrigerator.
■ Freeze: Not suitable.
■ Microwave: Not suitable.

GARLIC CHICKEN ON CRISP CROUTES WITH CREAM SAUCE

2½ tablespoons butter
2½ tablespoons olive oil
2 cloves garlic, minced
¼ cup lemon juice
**4 boneless, skinless chicken
     breast halves**
8 slices white bread
¼ cup olive oil, extra

CREAM SAUCE
2 tablespoons (¼ stick) butter
½ cup dry white wine
2 teaspoons French mustard
1¼ cups heavy cream
¼ cup grated fresh Parmesan cheese
1 tablespoon cornstarch
1½ tablespoons water
2½ tablespoons chopped fresh chives
**2½ tablespoons chopped
     fresh parsley**

Heat butter and oil in pan, add garlic and juice. Add chicken to pan, cook until tender; keep warm.

Cut a 3½ inch round from each bread slice. Heat extra oil in clean pan, add bread in batches, cook until well browned and crisp; drain on absorbent paper.

Just before serving, slice chicken, place on croutes, top with cream sauce.

Cream Sauce: Heat butter in pan, stir in wine, mustard, cream and cheese, cook, stirring, 2 minutes. Stir in blended cornstarch and water, stir over heat until sauce boils and thickens. Remove from heat, stir in herbs.

Serves 4.

■ Chicken best cooked just before serving. Croutes can be made 3 hours ahead.
■ Storage: Cooled croutes in airtight container.
■ Freeze: Not suitable.
■ Microwave: Sauce suitable.

CAMEMBERT CHICKEN KIEV

6 boneless, skinless chicken
    breast halves
6½oz camembert cheese, chopped
¾ cup (1½ sticks) butter, softened
2 cloves garlic, minced
1 tablespoon chopped fresh oregano
all-purpose flour
1 egg, lightly beaten
¼ cup milk
packaged, unseasoned bread crumbs
oil for deep-frying

Using meat mallet, gently pound chicken between sheets of plastic wrap until thin. Beat cheese, butter, garlic and oregano in small bowl with electric mixer until just combined. Place one-sixth of the filling evenly along center of each chicken fillet. Fold in sides of fillets, roll up firmly, place seam-side-down on tray, cover, refrigerate 1 hour or until filling is firm.

Toss rolls in flour, shake away excess flour. Dip in combined egg and milk, then bread crumbs to coat evenly.

Just before serving, deep-fry rolls 2 at a time in hot oil until cooked through.

Serves 6.

■ Recipe can be prepared 2 days ahead.
■ Storage: Covered, in refrigerator.
■ Freeze: Uncooked rolls suitable.
■ Microwave: Not suitable.

LEFT: From left: Quail with Almond Rice Seasoning and Grapes, Ginger Wine Duck with Orange Dumplings.
ABOVE: From left: Garlic Chicken on Crisp Croutes with Cream Sauce, Camembert Chicken Kiev.

ROCK CORNISH HENS WITH MINTED FRESH BERRY SAUCE

¼ cup raspberry jam
2½ tablespoons fresh orange juice
1 teaspoon light soy sauce
2 x 1lb Rock Cornish hens, halved
2½ tablespoons mint jelly, strained
2½ tablespoons olive oil
1 tablespoon red wine vinegar
7oz blueberries
7oz raspberries

Combine jam, juice and sauce in bowl, stir until smooth. Place hens in shallow dish, pour over jam mixture, cover, refrigerate several hours or overnight, turning occasionally.

Whisk jelly, oil and vinegar together in bowl, add berries, cover, stand 3 hours.

Just before serving, drain hens, reserve marinade. Place hens cut-side-down on wire rack in roasting pan, bake in 350°F oven about 35 minutes or until well browned and tender.

Bring reserved marinade to boil in pan, add berry mixture, cook gently, without stirring, until heated through. Serve hens with berry sauce.

Serves 4.

■ Hens can be prepared a day ahead.
■ Storage: Covered, in refrigerator.
■ Freeze: Not suitable.
■ Microwave: Sauce suitable.

ROCK CORNISH HENS WITH RAISIN RICE

1 cup water
1 small chicken bouillon
  cube, crumbled
⅓ cup long-grain rice
1 tablespoon olive oil
1 onion, finely chopped
1 bunch (1¼lb) spinach,
  finely chopped
2½ tablespoons finely chopped dark
  seedless raisins
1 teaspoon grated orange zest
1 teaspoon chopped fresh rosemary
4 x 1lb Rock Cornish hens

ORANGE GLAZE
½ cup fresh orange juice
1 tablespoon honey
2 tablespoons light soy sauce
2 teaspoons fresh rosemary leaves
1 teaspoon cornstarch
1 tablespoon water

Combine water and bouillon cube in pan, bring to boil. Add rice, stir until boiling, simmer, covered, about 10 minutes or until almost all liquid is absorbed. Cool in pan.

Heat oil in pan, add onion, cook, stirring, until soft. Add spinach, cook, stirring, 1 minute. Remove from heat, stir in rice mixture, raisins, zest and rosemary; cool. Fill hens with mixture, secure openings with small skewers or toothpicks, tie legs together, tuck wings under.

Just before serving, place hens on wire rack in roasting pan. Bake, uncovered, in 350°F oven about 45 minutes or until well browned and tender. Serve hens with orange glaze.

Orange Glaze: Combine juice, honey, sauce and rosemary in pan. Stir in blended cornstarch and water. Stir over heat until sauce boils and thickens.

Serves 8.

■ Recipe can be prepared a day ahead.
■ Storage: Covered, in refrigerator.
■ Freeze: Not suitable.
■ Microwave: Glaze suitable.

THYME AND LEMON CHICKEN ROLLS WITH ALMOND CRUMBS

4 boneless, skinless chicken
  breast halves
4 slices pastrami
3½oz ricotta cheese
½ teaspoon dried thyme leaves
2 teaspoons lemon curd or cheese
2 teaspoons chopped fresh parsley
all-purpose flour
1 egg, lightly beaten
⅔ cup fresh bread crumbs
⅔ cup packaged ground almonds
oil for deep-frying

LEMON SAUCE
1 cup water
2 small chicken bouillon
  cubes, crumbled
1 tablespoon lemon curd or cheese
2 teaspoons cornstarch

Using meat mallet, gently pound chicken between sheets of plastic wrap until ⅛ inch thick. Place a slice of pastrami over wider end of each chicken fillet. Spread with combined cheese, thyme, lemon curd and parsley. Roll each fillet from wide end.

Toss each roll in flour, shake away excess flour. Dip into egg, then combined bread crumbs and almonds to coat. Place on tray, cover, refrigerate 20 minutes.

Just before serving, deep-fry rolls in hot oil until lightly browned, drain on absorbent paper. Place rolls on baking sheet, bake in 350°F oven about 20 minutes or until cooked through. Stand rolls on absorbent paper 1 minute before cutting. Serve sliced chicken rolls with lemon sauce.

Lemon Sauce: Combine ¾ cup of the water, bouillon cubes and lemon curd in small pan. Stir in blended cornstarch and remaining water. Stir over heat until sauce

boils and thickens slightly, simmer, uncovered, 1 minute.

Serves 4.

- ■ Rolls can be prepared 2 days ahead. Sauce best prepared just before serving.
- ■ Storage: Rolls, covered, in refrigerator.
- ■ Freeze: Uncooked filled rolls suitable.
- ■ Microwave: Sauce suitable.

LEFT: Rock Cornish Hen with Minted Fresh Berry Sauce.
ABOVE: From top left: Rock Cornish Hen with Raisin Rice, Thyme and Lemon Chicken Rolls with Almond Crumbs, Broiled Paprika Quail with Beet Glaze.

BROILED PAPRIKA QUAIL WITH BEET GLAZE

8 quail
2½ tablespoons vegetable oil
¼ teaspoon paprika

BEET GLAZE
2 teaspoons grated gingerroot
1 tablespoon lemon juice
1 clove garlic, minced
1 tablespoon dark brown sugar
1½ cups water
2½ tablespoons cranberry sauce
2½ tablespoons cornstarch
¼ cup water, extra
5oz canned beet slices, drained

Brush quail evenly with combined oil and paprika. Tie legs together, cover legs with foil. Broil quail until well browned and cooked through, brushing with oil and paprika mixture during cooking. Serve broiled quail with beet glaze.

Beet Glaze: Combine gingerroot, juice, garlic, sugar and water in pan. Stir over heat until sugar is dissolved. Bring to boil, simmer, uncovered, 2 minutes; strain. Return strained glaze to pan, stir in cranberry sauce and blended cornstarch and extra water. Stir over heat until mixture boils and thickens; remove from heat. Cut beet slices into strips, stir into glaze, stir until beets are heated through.

Serves 8.

- ■ Quail best cooked just before serving. Sauce can be made a day ahead.
- ■ Storage: Covered, in refrigerator.
- ■ Freeze: Not suitable.
- ■ Microwave: Not suitable.

CHICKEN WELLINGTONS WITH REDCURRANT SAUCE

¼ cup vegetable oil
8 large boneless, skinless chicken
    breast halves
2 tablespoons (¼ stick) butter
1 onion, chopped
2 cloves garlic, minced
¾lb mushrooms, chopped
½ teaspoon cracked black
    peppercorns
⅓ cup chopped fresh parsley
12 sheets phyllo pastry
3oz (¾ stick) butter, melted, extra

REDCURRANT SAUCE
3 oranges
1 cup port wine
1 cup redcurrant jelly
1 teaspoon French mustard
½ teaspoon cracked black
    peppercorns
1 small chicken bouillon
    cube, crumbled
1½ tablespoons cornstarch
2½ tablespoons water

Heat oil in pan, add chicken in single layer, cook until lightly browned all over and tender, drain on absorbent paper; cool.

Heat butter in pan, add onion and garlic, cook, stirring, until onion is soft. Add mushrooms, cook, stirring, until mushrooms are soft and liquid has evaporated. Stir in peppercorns and parsley; cool.

Halve pastry crossways. Layer 3 halves together, brushing each with some of the butter. Spread layered pastry with one-eighth of the mushroom mixture. Top with a chicken fillet, fold in sides and roll up to form a parcel. Repeat with remaining pastry, butter, mushroom mixture and fillets. Place parcels on greased baking sheets, brush with remaining butter.

Just before serving, bake parcels in 350°F oven about 20 minutes or until pastry is well browned. Serve wellingtons with redcurrant sauce.

Redcurrant Sauce: Using vegetable peeler, cut colored peel from 1 orange. Cut peel into thin strips. Squeeze juice from oranges (you will need 2 cups of juice). Combine peel, juice, port, jelly, mustard, peppercorns and bouillon cube in pan. Bring to boil, simmer, uncovered, 10 minutes, stirring occasionally. Stir in blended cornstarch and water, stir until sauce boils and thickens.

Serves 8.

- Wellingtons can be prepared 6 hours ahead.
- Storage: Covered, in refrigerator.
- Freeze: Not suitable.
- Microwave: Not suitable.

BELOW: From left: Honeyed Duck with Wild Rice Seasoning, Chicken Wellingtons with Redcurrant Sauce.
BELOW RIGHT: Chicken and Sweet Potato Rolls with Piquant Sauce.

HONEYED DUCKS WITH WILD RICE SEASONING

2 x 2½lb ducks
2 tablespoons (¼ stick) butter, melted
2½ tablespoons honey

WILD RICE SEASONING
½ cup wild rice
⅓ cup long-grain rice
1 tablespoon butter
1 onion, chopped
2 cloves garlic, minced
2½oz mushrooms, chopped
2oz Brazil nuts, roughly chopped
2½ tablespoons chopped
    fresh parsley
1 teaspoon grated orange zest
½ cup fresh orange juice
½ teaspoon ground all-spice

BRANDIED ORANGE SAUCE
1 large chicken bouillon
    cube, crumbled
1½ cups water
⅓ cup honey
1 cup fresh orange juice
½ cup brandy
2½ tablespoons cornstarch
¼ cup water, extra

Fill ducks with wild rice seasoning; secure openings with skewers, tie legs together, tuck wings under.

Prick skin with fork to release fat during cooking, place ducks on wire rack in roasting pan, add a little water to pan. Brush combined butter and honey over ducks. Bake, uncovered, in 350°F oven about 2 hours or until well browned and tender, brushing occasionally with remaining honey mixture. Prick skins twice more during cooking.

Cover legs, wings and breasts with foil during cooking if ducks are browning too quickly. Serve ducks with hot brandied orange sauce.

Wild Rice Seasoning: Add wild rice to large pan of boiling water, boil, uncovered, 15 minutes. Add long-grain rice, boil, uncovered, 12 minutes; drain.

Heat butter in pan, add onion and garlic, cook, stirring, until onion is soft. Add mushrooms, cook, stirring, 2 minutes. Combine rice mixture and mushroom mixture in large bowl, stir in remaining ingredients; mix well.

Brandied Orange Sauce: Combine bouillon cube, water, honey, juice and brandy in pan. Bring to boil, simmer, uncovered, about 10 minutes or until reduced by one-third. Stir in blended cornstarch and extra water, stir over heat until sauce boils and thickens.

Serves 8.

■ Ducks can be prepared a day ahead. Sauce best made just before serving.
■ Storage: Covered, in refrigerator.
■ Freeze: Not suitable.
■ Microwave: Sauce suitable.

CHICKEN AND SWEET POTATO ROLLS WITH PIQUANT SAUCE

4 whole chicken breasts
1 tablespoon lemon juice
2 teaspoons dark brown sugar
1 tablespoon vegetable oil
pinch ground nutmeg

FILLING
½lb sweet potato, finely chopped
2 green onions, finely chopped
2 teaspoons dark brown sugar
½ teaspoon grated orange zest
1 teaspoon lemon juice
1oz cooked ham, chopped
2½ tablespoons chopped unsalted
    roasted cashews

PIQUANT SAUCE
1 cup dry white wine
1 cup fresh orange juice
⅓ cup lemon juice
1 tablespoon dark brown sugar
1½ tablespoons marmalade
1½ tablespoons cornstarch
1½ tablespoons water

Bone and skin chicken, keeping fillets joined in center. Using meat mallet, gently pound fillets between sheets of plastic wrap until ¼ inch thick. Spread with filling, roll up tightly, secure with skewers. Place rolls in shallow dish, pour over combined juice, sugar, oil and nutmeg, cover, refrigerate several hours or overnight.

Just before serving, drain rolls, reserve liquid. Place rolls onto baking sheet, bake in 350°F oven about 20 minutes, brushing frequently with reserved liquid, or until browned and just tender. Stand 5 minutes before slicing; serve with piquant sauce.

Filling: Boil, steam or microwave sweet potato until soft, drain, mash in bowl; cool. Stir remaining ingredients into sweet potato; mix well.

Piquant Sauce: Combine wine, juices, sugar and marmalade in pan, stir, without boiling, until sugar is dissolved. Bring to boil, simmer, uncovered, about 5 minutes or until reduced by one-third. Stir in blended cornstarch and water, stir over heat until sauce boils and thickens.

Serves 8.

■ Rolls can be prepared a day ahead.
■ Storage: Covered, in refrigerator.
■ Freeze: Uncooked rolls suitable.
■ Microwave: Sweet potato suitable.

CHICKEN, PEPPER AND APPLE PASTRIES

**8 boneless, skinless chicken
    breast halves**
all-purpose flour
1½ tablespoons butter
1 tablespoon olive oil
⅓ cup apple jelly
12 sheets phyllo pastry
2½ tablespoons butter, melted, extra
1 tablespoon olive oil, extra

FILLING
1 tablespoon olive oil
1 red bell pepper, finely chopped
1 clove garlic, minced
1 tablespoon chopped fresh dill
1 green onion, finely chopped
3½oz feta cheese, crumbled
4 pitted black olives, finely chopped

Toss chicken fillets in flour, shake away excess flour. Heat butter and oil in pan, add fillets in batches, cook until browned all over, drain on absorbent paper; cool.

Spread fillets with jelly, top with filling. Halve pastry crossways, layer 3 half sheets together, brushing each with some of the combined extra butter and extra oil. Place 1 fillet at narrow end of layered pastry, fold in sides and roll up; brush with butter mixture. Repeat with remaining pastry, butter mixture and fillets. Place pastries on greased baking sheet.

Just before serving, bake pastries in 350°F oven about 35 minutes or until lightly browned and cooked through.

Filling: Heat oil in pan, add pepper, cook, stirring, until pepper is soft. Remove from heat, stir in garlic; cool. Stir in remaining ingredients; mix well.

Serves 8.

- Can be prepared a day ahead.
- Storage: Covered, in refrigerator.
- Freeze: Not suitable.
- Microwave: Filling suitable.

TURKEY WITH LYCHEES

6lb turkey
2oz sliced cooked ham
¼ cup (½ stick) butter, melted

LYCHEE SEASONING
14oz can lychees
1lb ground pork and veal
½ cup shredded coconut
¾ cup fresh bread crumbs
1 teaspoon grated lime zest
1 tablespoon lime juice
1 egg, lightly beaten
1 tablespoon chopped fresh mint
1 teaspoon chopped fresh parsley

LYCHEE SAUCE
2 cups water
1 large chicken bouillon
  cube, crumbled
2½ tablespoons dry sherry
2½ tablespoons cornstarch
2½ tablespoons water, extra
1 tablespoon chopped fresh parsley

Bone turkey following instructions in "Pre-Cooking Preparations" at the back of this book. Spread turkey skin-side-down on bench, fold 1 leg over the other, secure with skewer. Spoon half the lychee seasoning along center of turkey, top with ham, cover with remaining seasoning.

Roll turkey from breast side towards legs over seasoning, secure with skewers, then with kitchen string at 1 inch intervals. Brush turkey with butter, place on wire rack in roasting pan. Cover turkey with foil, bake in 350°F oven 2¼ hours, basting occasionally with pan juices. Remove foil, bake further 15 minutes or until tender. Serve sliced turkey with lychee sauce.

Lychee Seasoning: Drain lychees, reserve syrup for sauce; chop lychees. Combine lychees, pork and veal, coconut, bread crumbs, zest, juice, egg, mint and parsley in bowl; mix well.

Lychee Sauce: Combine reserved lychee syrup, water, bouillon cube and sherry in pan. Bring to boil, boil, uncovered, 5 minutes. Stir in blended cornstarch and extra water, stir over heat until sauce boils and thickens; add parsley.

Serves 10.

- Turkey can be prepared a day ahead.
- Storage: Covered, in refrigerator.
- Freeze: Uncooked seasoned
- turkey suitable.
- Microwave: Not suitable.

GARLIC MUSTARD ROCK CORNISH HENS WITH POLENTA

3 x 1lb Rock Cornish hens, halved
1 tablespoon olive oil
3 cloves garlic, minced
1 teaspoon dried oregano leaves
1 teaspoon brown mustard seeds
2½ tablespoons dry red wine
¼ cup French salad dressing

POLENTA
1½ tablespoons butter
½ cup yellow cornmeal
1¾ cups water
2 small chicken bouillon
  cubes, crumbled
1 egg, lightly beaten
⅔ cup grated fresh Parmesan cheese
all-purpose flour
oil for shallow-frying

Combine hens, oil, garlic, oregano, seeds and wine in bowl, cover; refrigerate several hours or overnight.

Just before serving, place hens cut-side-down on wire rack in roasting pan, bake in 375°F oven about 35 minutes or until well browned and tender. Serve hens with polenta; drizzle with dressing.

Polenta: Line 3½ inch x 10½ inch baking pan with plastic wrap. Heat butter in pan, add cornmeal, water and bouillon cubes. Stir until mixture boils, simmer, covered, about 20 minutes, stirring occasionally,

until mixture is thickened. Remove from heat, stir in egg and cheese. Spread mixture into prepared pan; smooth surface. Refrigerate, uncovered, 1 hour.

Turn polenta onto board, cut polenta into ½ inch fingers, toss in flour, shake away excess flour. Shallow-fry polenta in batches in pan until well browned on both sides; drain on absorbent paper.

Serves 6.

- Recipe can be prepared a day ahead.
- Storage: Covered, in refrigerator.
- Freeze: Not suitable.
- Microwave: Not suitable.

LEFT: From top: Turkey with Lychees, Chicken, Pepper and Apple Pastries.
ABOVE: Garlic Mustard Rock Cornish Hens with Polenta.

PEPPER PASTA WITH DUCK SAUSAGE

2 cups all-purpose flour
2 teaspoons seasoned pepper
3 eggs
1 teaspoon water, approximately

TOMATO SAUCE
14½oz can tomatoes
1 cup water
2½ tablespoons dry red wine
1 small chicken bouillon
     cube, crumbled
1 cup fresh basil leaves

DUCK SAUSAGE
3½lb duck
2 tablespoons (¼ stick) butter
1 onion, chopped
¼ teaspoon chili powder
½ teaspoon paprika
1 egg white
1 cup (2½oz) fresh bread crumbs
1½ tablespoons oil

Mix flour, pepper and eggs in bowl or processor until mixture forms a ball, adding a little water, if necessary (mixture should be firm but not flaky). Knead dough on lightly floured surface about 10 minutes or until smooth. If making by hand, cover dough, refrigerate 20 minutes. Roll dough on lightly floured surface until about ⅛ inch thick.

If using pasta machine, cut dough in half, roll each half through thickest setting of machine, fold dough in half. Repeat rolling and folding, gradually decreasing setting on machine until dough is about ⅛ inch thick. Cut pasta evenly into 1¼ inch strips.

Just before serving, add pasta to large pan of boiling water, boil, uncovered, about 5 minutes or until just tender; drain. Combine hot pasta, hot tomato sauce and duck sausage in bowl.

Tomato Sauce: Combine undrained crushed tomatoes, water, wine and bouillon cube in pan. Bring to boil, simmer, uncovered, about 10 minutes or until mixture thickens slightly; stir in fresh basil leaves.

Duck Sausage: Remove skin and fat from duck, remove meat from bones, discard skin, fat and bones; chop the duck meat roughly.

Heat butter in pan, add onion, chili and paprika, cook, stirring, until onion is soft. Process duck meat, onion mixture and egg white until smooth. Transfer mixture to bowl, stir in bread crumbs.

Divide mixture into 3 portions. Spoon 1 portion of mixture along center of piece of plastic wrap. Fold wrap around mixture, forming sausage shape about 1¼ inch in diameter. Repeat with remaining mixture. Wrap each roll in foil, twist ends to seal. Add rolls to large pan of simmering water, simmer, covered, 10 minutes. Remove rolls from water, stand 5 minutes before unwrapping; cut sausage evenly into ½ inch slices.

Heat oil in pan, add sausage slices, cook until lightly browned on both sides; drain on absorbent paper.

Serves 4.

■ Pasta best prepared just before serving. Sausage and sauce can be made a day ahead.
■ Storage: Covered, in refrigerator.
■ Freeze: Uncooked sausage and sauce suitable.
■ Microwave: Pasta and sauce suitable.

TURKEY BREAST WITH CORNBREAD SEASONING

2lb boneless turkey breast half
all-purpose flour
1 cup cranberry sauce
1 teaspoon cornstarch
1 teaspoon water

CORNBREAD SEASONING
⅓ cup cornmeal
½ cup self-rising flour
1 tablespoon sugar
¼ cup milk
¼ cup water
1 egg, lightly beaten
4½oz canned whole-kernel corn,
     drained
2 tablespoons (¼ stick) butter
1 small fresh red chili pepper,
     chopped
1 stalk celery, chopped
4 green onions, chopped
1 egg yolk
¼ teaspoon dried mixed herbs

Trim any excess fat from turkey fillet, cut a deep, horizontal pocket in center without cutting all the way through. Fill pocket with cornbread seasoning; secure opening with skewers.

Dust fillet in flour, shake away excess flour. Place fillet in oven bag; secure bag with strip provided. Pierce bag as directed on oven bag package. Place fillet in roasting pan, bake in 350°F oven about 1 hour or until lightly browned and tender. Remove fillet from bag, keep warm. Reserve ¼ cup juices in bag for sauce.

Combine reserved juices and cranberry sauce in pan. Stir in blended cornstarch and water, stir over heat until sauce boils and thickens. Serve sliced fillet with cranberry sauce.

Cornbread Seasoning: Lightly grease 3½ inch x 10½ inch baking pan, line base with paper; grease paper. Combine cornmeal, flour and sugar in bowl, stir in combined milk, water, egg and corn. Spoon mixture into prepared pan. Bake in 350°F oven about 40 minutes or until firm; cool in pan. Crumble half the cornbread into bowl (freeze remaining half for another use).

Heat butter in pan, add chili, celery and onions, cook, stirring, until celery is soft.

Remove from heat, cool slightly, stir in egg yolk and herbs. Add celery mixture to cornbread; mix well.

Serves 8.

- Recipe can be made 2 days ahead.
- Storage: Covered, in refrigerator.
- Freeze: Seasoned fillet suitable.
- Microwave: Sauce suitable.

HAM, CHICKEN AND BLUE CHEESE SACHETS

8 boneless, skinless chicken
breast halves
8 slices cooked ham
all-purpose flour
2 eggs, lightly beaten
1½ cups (3½oz) fresh bread crumbs
⅓ cup chopped fresh parsley
2½ tablespoons vegetable oil
1½ tablespoons butter

FILLING
½lb blue vein cheese, crumbled
2 tablespoons dry white wine

Using meat mallet, gently pound chicken between sheets of plastic wrap until thin. Place a slice of ham on each fillet, divide filling along center of ham slices. Fold in sides of each fillet, fold in half to enclose filling. Place sachets on tray, cover, refrigerate 20 minutes. Carefully toss sachets in flour, shake away excess flour. Dip into eggs, then combined bread crumbs and parsley.
Just before serving, heat oil and butter

in pan, add sachets, cook until lightly browned all over. Place sachets on baking sheet, bake in 350°F oven about 15 minutes or until chicken is tender.
Filling: Mash cheese and wine in bowl until combined.

Serves 8.

- Sachets can be prepared a day ahead.
- Storage: Covered, in refrigerator.
- Freeze: Uncooked sachets suitable.
- Microwave: Not suitable.

ROAST DUCK WITH CHERRY ORANGE SEASONING

14 oz can sweet red cherries
3¼lb duck

CHERRY ORANGE SEASONING
1 tablespoon butter
1 clove garlic, minced
2½ tablespoons slivered almonds
2 teaspoons grated orange zest
¼ teaspoon ground cumin
3 cups (7oz) fresh bread crumbs
1 egg, lightly beaten
1 tablespoon fresh orange juice

SAUCE
1 tablespoon cornstarch
¼ cup fresh orange juice
½ teaspoon sugar
1 small chicken bouillon
cube, crumbled

Drain cherries, reserve syrup and half the cherries for sauce. Cut remaining cherries

in half; reserve halves for seasoning.

Fill duck with cherry orange seasoning, secure opening with skewers, tie legs together, tuck wings under.

Prick skin with fork to release fat during cooking, place duck on wire rack in roasting pan, add a little water to pan. Bake in 350°F oven about 2 hours or until well browned and tender. Prick skin twice more during cooking.
Cherry Orange Seasoning: Heat butter in pan, add garlic, almonds, zest and cumin, cook, stirring, until almonds are lightly browned. Remove from heat, stir in reserved halved cherries, bread crumbs, egg and juice.
Sauce: Combine blended cornstarch and juice with sugar, bouillon cube, reserved cherries and syrup in pan. Stir over heat until sauce boils and thickens.

Serves 4.

- Duck can be prepared a day ahead. Sauce can be made a day ahead.
- Storage: Covered, in refrigerator.
- Freeze: Uncooked seasoned duck suitable.
- Microwave: Sauce suitable.

ABOVE: Clockwise from top left: Roast Duck with Cherry Orange Seasoning, Turkey Breast with Cornbread Seasoning, Ham, Chicken and Blue Cheese Sachets
LEFT: Pepper Pasta with Duck Sausage.

ROASTED CHICKEN WITH CHERRY SEASONING

3¼lb chicken

CHERRY SEASONING
14oz can pitted black cherries
2½ cups (6oz) fresh bread crumbs
1½ tablespoons horseradish cream
1 teaspoon grated lemon zest
1 egg, lightly beaten
1 stalk celery, chopped
1 tablespoon chopped fresh parsley

SAUCE
2 teaspoons cornstarch
2 teaspoons water
2 teaspoons light soy sauce
2 green onions, chopped

Remove excess fat from chicken. Fill chicken with cherry seasoning, secure opening with skewer, tie legs together, tuck wings under.

Place chicken on wire rack in roasting pan. Bake in 350°F oven about 1½ hours or until well browned and tender. Serve chicken with warm sauce.

Cherry Seasoning: Drain cherries, reserve ¾ cup syrup for sauce. Combine cherries and remaining ingredients in bowl; mix well.
Sauce: Blend cornstarch with water, combine with reserved syrup, sauce and onions in pan. Stir over heat until sauce boils and thickens slightly.

Serves 4.

■ Recipe best made close to serving.
■ Freeze: Not suitable.
■ Microwave: Sauce suitable.

ARTICHOKES AND PASTRAMI STIR-FRY WITH CHICKEN

2½ tablespoons olive oil
8 chicken thigh cutlets
14oz can artichoke hearts, drained
2 onions, sliced
7oz sliced pastrami, chopped
1 teaspoon cracked coriander seeds
½ cup water
**½ small chicken bouillon
    cube, crumbled**
¼ cup lemon juice
2 teaspoons chopped fresh dill

Heat oil in pan, add chicken in batches, cook until lightly browned but not cooked through; drain on absorbent paper.

Cut artichokes into quarters. Add onions to same pan, cook, stirring, until soft and lightly browned. Stir in pastrami and seeds, cook, stirring, 5 minutes.

Return chicken to pan, add artichokes, water, bouillon cube and juice. Bring to boil, simmer, covered, about 25 minutes or until chicken is tender, stirring occasionally. Stir in dill just before serving.

Serves 4.

- Recipe can be made a day ahead.
- Storage: Covered, in refrigerator.
- Freeze: Not suitable.
- Microwave: Not suitable.

CHICKEN CORDON BLEU WITH SHERRY CREAM SAUCE

8 small boneless, skinless chicken breast halves
4 small slices cooked ham
4 slices Swiss cheese
all-purpose flour
1 egg, lightly beaten
2½ tablespoons milk
1 cup (3½oz) packaged, unseasoned bread crumbs
1 cup (2½oz) fresh bread crumbs
1½ tablespoons grated lemon zest
¼ cup (½ stick) butter
¼ cup vegetable oil

SHERRY CREAM SAUCE
2 tablespoons (¼ stick) butter
1 clove garlic, minced
1 cup water
1 small chicken bouillon cube, crumbled
½ cup dry sherry
¼ cup heavy cream
2 teaspoons all-purpose flour
1½ tablespoons chopped fresh parsley

Using meat mallet, gently pound chicken fillets between sheets of plastic wrap until ¼ inch thick, trim edges. Place a slice of ham on each of 4 chicken fillets, top with the slices of cheese, then remaining fillets; press firmly together.

Carefully coat fillets with flour, shake away excess flour. Dip into combined egg and milk, then combined bread crumbs and zest, pressing mixture on firmly. Place on tray, cover; refrigerate 1 hour.

Just before serving, heat butter and oil in pan, add chicken, cook until well browned and tender; drain on absorbent paper. Serve hot chicken with hot sherry cream sauce.

Sherry Cream Sauce: Heat butter in pan, add garlic, cook, stirring, until fragrant. Add water, bouillon cube and sherry, bring to boil, simmer, uncovered, until reduced by half. Stir in blended cream and flour, stir until sauce boils and thickens, simmer 1 minute. Stir in parsley.

Serves 4.

- Recipe can be prepared a day ahead.
- Storage: Covered, in refrigerator.
- Freeze: Uncooked chicken suitable.
- Microwave: Sauce suitable.

CURRIED CHICKEN AND SWEET POTATO ROULADE

7oz white sweet potato, chopped
1½ tablespoons olive oil
1 onion, chopped
¾lb chicken thighs, boned, skinned, chopped
½ teaspoon turmeric
¼ teaspoon garam masala
¼ teaspoon ground cumin
⅔ cup canned unsweetened coconut milk
1 tablespoon smooth peanut butter
1½ tablespoons chopped fresh cilantro
¼ cup (½ stick) butter
⅓ cup all-purpose flour
1 cup water
1 small chicken bouillon cube, crumbled
4 eggs, separated
1 tablespoon chopped fresh mint
¾ cup grated fresh Parmesan cheese

Grease 10 inch x 12 inch jelly-roll pan, line base with paper; grease paper. Add sweet potato to pan of boiling water, simmer, covered, until tender, cool in water.

Heat oil in pan, add onion and chicken, cook, stirring, until chicken is lightly browned. Stir in spices, milk and peanut butter. Bring to boil, simmer, uncovered, 15 minutes, stir in cilantro. Blend or process mixture until smooth, stir in drained sweet potato; keep warm.

Melt butter in pan, stir in flour, stir over heat until bubbling. Remove from heat, gradually stir in water and bouillon cube, stir over heat until sauce boils and thickens; cool slightly. Stir in egg yolks, mint and cheese, transfer mixture to large bowl.

Beat egg whites in small bowl with electric mixer until soft peaks form, fold lightly into cheese mixture. Pour mixture into prepared pan, bake in 400°F oven about 12 minutes or until puffed and well browned. Turn onto wire rack covered with tea-towel, carefully remove lining paper. Spread evenly with chicken mixture. Gently roll roulade from long side using tea-towel to lift and guide. Serve roulade hot, cut into slices.

Serves 6.

- Recipe best made just before serving.
- Freeze: Not suitable.
- Microwave: Not suitable.

LEFT: Clockwise from top: Roasted Chicken with Cherry Seasoning, Chicken Cordon Bleu with Sherry Cream Sauce, Artichokes and Pastrami Stir-Fry with Chicken.
ABOVE: Curried Chicken and Sweet Potato Roulade.

CHICKEN BALLOTINES WITH LENTIL CHILI SAUCE

**6 chicken marylands (thighs
    with legs)**
2½ tablespoons butter
1 onion, finely chopped
7oz ground chicken
1 tablespoon heavy cream
1 tablespoon dry sherry
¼ cup chopped pistachios
1 green onion, chopped

LENTIL CHILI SAUCE
2½ tablespoons vegetable oil
1 onion, finely chopped
**1 small fresh red chili pepper,
    finely chopped**
1½ cups (10oz) red lentils
**1 large chicken bouillon cube,
    crumbled**
2 teaspoons brown vinegar
3 cups water
1½ tablespoons tomato paste

Starting from thigh end of each chicken maryland, run sharp knife point along thigh and along leg, exposing bones. Remove a little flesh from end of thigh bone. Holding thigh bone, scrape flesh away from bone. Cut through joint only, not through flesh. Remove thigh bone.

Holding thin end of leg, scrape flesh back to joint, remove bone. Flesh should be intact.

Heat butter in pan, add onion, cook, stirring, until onion is soft; cool. Combine onion, chicken, cream, sherry, nuts and green onion in bowl. Place each chicken piece skin-side-down on bench, place quarter of mixture on each piece, wrap chicken around mixture to enclose. Secure with small skewers or toothpicks. **Just before serving,** place ballotines on wire rack in roasting pan, bake, uncovered, in 350°F oven about 50 minutes or until lightly browned and cooked

through. Remove skewers, serve with hot lentil chili sauce.
Lentil Chili Sauce: Heat oil in pan, add onion and chili, cook, stirring, until onion is soft. Add remaining ingredients, bring to boil, simmer, covered, about 15 minutes or until lentils are soft.

Serves 6.
- Recipe can be prepared a day ahead.
- Storage: Covered, in refrigerator.
- Freeze: Uncooked ballotines suitable.
- Microwave: Sauce suitable.

DUCK WITH GARLIC CHICKEN SEASONING

2½ tablespoons oil
1 onion, finely chopped
4 cloves garlic, minced
½lb ground chicken
2 teaspoons heavy cream
**7oz can sliced water
    chestnuts, drained**
3 whole duck breasts, boned

MANGO SAUCE
2 x 14oz cans sliced mango
**1 small fresh red chili
    pepper, chopped**
**1 small chicken bouillon
    cube, crumbled**
1 onion, sliced
2½ tablespoons apricot jam

Heat oil in pan, add onion and garlic, cook, stirring, until onion is soft. Combine onion mixture, chicken, cream and chestnuts in bowl, cover, refrigerate 1 hour.

Cut wings from duck if still attached.

Trim excess fat from duck skin, leaving skin intact. Place duck skin-side-down on bench, spread out flaps of skin.

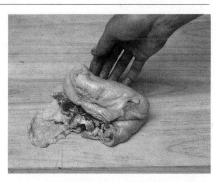

Place one-third of the chicken mixture on each fillet, roll up firmly, secure with kitchen string at 1 inch intervals. Place rolls on wire rack in roasting pan, bake, uncovered, in 350°F oven about 1 hour or until browned and tender. Stand 10 minutes, cut into slices. Serve hot with mango sauce.
Mango Sauce: Combine undrained mangoes with remaining ingredients in pan, bring to boil, simmer, covered, about 15 minutes or until onion is soft; cool. Blend or process sauce until smooth, return to pan, stir until heated through.

Serves 6.
- Rolls can be prepared a day ahead. Sauce can be made 2 days ahead.
- Storage: Covered, in refrigerator.
- Freeze: Uncooked seasoned duck suitable.
- Microwave: Sauce suitable.

CHICKEN WITH WILD RICE AND FRUIT

¼ cup vegetable oil
8 chicken thighs, boned, skinned
1 onion, chopped
5oz wild rice
4 cups water
**2 small chicken bouillon
    cubes, crumbled**
1 bouquet garni
1 tablespoon white mustard seeds
¼ cup chopped dried apricots
¼ cup golden raisins
¼ cup currants
1½ tablespoons butter
1 tablespoon sugar
12 pearl onions

Heat oil in pan. Add chicken in single layer, cook until browned all over, remove from pan.

Add chopped onion and rice to pan, cook, stirring, 2 minutes. Stir in half the water, bouillon cubes, bouquet garni and seeds. Bring to boil, simmer, covered, 20 minutes. Stir in dried fruit, chicken and 1 cup of the remaining water. Transfer mixture to ovenproof dish, cover, bake in 350°F oven about 30 minutes or until chicken is tender.

Combine butter, sugar and remaining water in pan. Bring to boil, add pearl onions, boil, uncovered, about 5 minutes or until onions are lightly browned and cooked through.

Add onion mixture to dish, bring to boil, simmer, uncovered, until most of the liquid is evaporated. Remove and discard bouquet garni.

Serves 4.

- ▆ Recipe can be made a day ahead.
- ▆ Storage: Covered, in refrigerator.
- ▆ Freeze: Uncooked mixture suitable.
- ▆ Microwave: Not suitable.

LEFT: Clockwise from top: Chicken with Wild Rice and Fruit, Chicken Ballotines with Lentil Chili Sauce, Duck with Garlic Chicken Seasoning.

TURKEY VEGETABLE PUFFS

**1lb boneless, skinless turkey
    breast piece**
¼ cup light soy sauce
1 teaspoon five-spice powder
1½ tablespoons lemon juice
10 spears fresh asparagus
3½oz green beans
1 carrot
¼ cup vegetable oil
1 onion, chopped
1 clove garlic, minced
1 red bell pepper, chopped
5oz broccoli, chopped
¼ cup oyster-flavored sauce
1 cup water
1½ tablespoons tomato paste
1 tablespoon cornstarch
½ cup dry sherry
CHOUX PASTRY
1 cup water
3oz (¾ stick) butter
¾ cup all-purpose flour
4 eggs
1 egg, lightly beaten, extra

Combine sliced turkey, soy sauce, spice and juice in bowl, cover, refrigerate several hours or overnight.

Cut asparagus and beans into 2 inch lengths. Cut carrot into thin sticks. Heat oil in pan, add onion and garlic, cook, stirring, until onion is soft. Add turkey mixture, cook, stirring, until lightly browned.

Add asparagus, beans, carrot, pepper and broccoli, cook, stirring, 2 minutes. Stir in oyster sauce, water, paste and blended cornstarch and sherry. Stir until mixture boils and thickens, simmer, uncovered, about 2 minutes or until turkey is tender.

Split puffs horizontally, spoon in hot filling, replace tops, serve immediately.

Choux Pastry: Lightly grease 2 baking sheets, mark 4 x 3 inch circles 2 inches apart on each sheet.

Combine water and butter in pan, bring to boil, stirring, until butter is melted. Add sifted flour all at once, stir vigorously over heat until mixture leaves side of pan and forms a smooth ball.

Transfer mixture to small bowl of electric mixer (or food processor). Add eggs 1 at a time, beat on low speed until smooth after each addition.

Spoon mixture into piping bag fitted with ½ inch star tube. Starting from center, pipe mixture thickly into each marked circle on prepared baking sheets until circles are covered. Lightly brush pastry with extra egg. Bake in 400°F oven 10 minutes, reduce heat to 350°F, bake further 5 minutes or until puffs are lightly browned and crisp. Cool on wire rack.

Serves 8.

- Puffs and filling can be made separately a day ahead.
- Storage: Puffs, in airtight container. Filling, covered, in refrigerator.
- Freeze: Unfilled puffs suitable.
- Microwave: Not suitable.

CHICKEN WITH RED PEPPERS

3¼lb chicken
8 slices (about 2½oz) prosciutto
FILLING
2 bunches (2½lb) spinach
2 tablespoons (¼ stick) butter
2 leeks, chopped
3½oz feta cheese, crumbled
pinch ground nutmeg
SAUCE
1½ tablespoons olive oil
1 onion, chopped
2 red bell peppers, chopped
½ cup dry white wine
14½oz can tomatoes
¼ teaspoon sugar
¼ cup sour cream
1 tablespoon chopped fresh tarragon

Bone chicken following instructions in "Pre-Cooking Preparations" at the back of this book. Place chicken skin-side-down on bench, cover with prosciutto, spoon filling down center; roll up.

Place chicken onto piece of greased foil, roll chicken in foil, twist ends tightly.

Place roll on wire rack in roasting pan, bake in 350°F oven about 1 hour or until tender, stand 10 minutes. Serve chicken sliced with sauce.

Filling: Place spinach in pan, cover, cook gently until wilted, drain, rinse under cold water. Squeeze excess water from spinach, chop spinach, place in bowl. Heat butter in pan, add leeks, cook, stirring, until soft. Add leeks, cheese and nutmeg to spinach; mix well.

Sauce: Heat oil in pan, add onion and peppers, cook, stirring, until vegetables are soft. Add wine, undrained crushed tomatoes and sugar, simmer, uncovered, about 30 minutes or until sauce is thickened slightly. Blend or process sauce, strain into pan. Reheat sauce, remove from heat, stir in cream and tarragon, stir until combined.

Serves 6.

- Chicken can be made 2 days ahead. Sauce best made just before serving.
- Storage: Covered, in refrigerator.
- Freeze: Uncooked filled chicken suitable.
- Microwave: Not suitable.

BAKED LIQUEUR CHICKEN

¼lb slices bacon
3 sprigs fresh thyme
2½lb chicken
2½ tablespoons butter
10 green onions, chopped
1 cup water
**1 small chicken bouillon
    cube, crumbled**
2½ tablespoons Creme de Cassis
2½ tablespoons heavy cream

Cut bacon into thin strips. Place thyme inside chicken. Tie legs together, tuck wings under. Heat half the butter in pan, add chicken to pan, cook until browned all over. Remove chicken to ovenproof dish.

Add remaining butter, onions and bacon to pan, cook, stirring, until onions are just soft, spoon into dish with chicken. Add water, bouillon cube and liqueur to pan, bring to boil, pour over chicken. Cover dish, bake in 350°F oven about 1¼ hours or until chicken is tender. Remove chicken from dish; keep warm.

Pour bacon mixture into pan, bring to boil, boil, uncovered, until liquid is reduced to about ½ cup. Add cream, stir until heated through, serve over chicken.

Serves 4.

■ Recipe can be made 2 hours ahead.
■ Storage: Covered, at room temperature.
■ Freeze: Suitable.
■ Microwave: Not suitable.

ROAST TURKEY WITH CASHEW SEASONING

10lb turkey
2½ tablespoons vegetable oil
1½ tablespoons mango chutney, finely chopped

CASHEW SEASONING
2 tablespoons (¼ stick) butter
1 small onion, chopped
1 clove garlic, minced
¼ teaspoon ground cardamom
¼ teaspoon ground cumin
1 cup (5oz) unroasted unsalted cashews
1 red bell pepper, chopped
1lb ground pork and veal
¼lb cooked ham, chopped
½ cup fresh bread crumbs
1½ tablespoons chopped fresh parsley
2 teaspoons chopped fresh chives
1 egg

MANGO SAUCE
2 (about 1lb) mangoes, chopped
1 cup pineapple juice
1 small chicken bouillon cube, crumbled
½ cup water
1 tablespoon all-purpose flour

Remove neck from inside turkey, wash turkey well, pat dry inside and out. Fill turkey with cashew seasoning, secure opening with skewers, tie legs together, tuck wings under. Place on wire rack in roasting pan; add a little water to pan.

Bake in 350°F oven about 4½ hours or until tender. Brush with combined oil and chutney after 4 hours. Cover legs, wings and breast with foil during cooking if turkey is browning too quickly.

Remove turkey to serving plate; reserve 1½ tablespoons of pan drippings for mango sauce. Serve turkey with sauce.
Cashew Seasoning: Melt butter in pan, add onion, garlic, cardamom and cumin, cook, stirring, until onion is soft. Add cashews and pepper, cook, stirring,

1 minute; cool. Combine remaining ingredients in large bowl, stir in cashew mixture; mix well.
Mango Sauce: Combine mangoes and juice in pan, cover, cook gently about 5 minutes or until pulpy. Stir in bouillon cube and water. Heat reserved pan drippings in separate pan, add flour, cook, stirring, until well browned. Remove from heat, gradually stir in mango mixture. Stir over heat until sauce boils and thickens.

Serves 12.

■ Recipe can be prepared a day ahead.
■ Storage: Covered, in refrigerator.
■ Freeze: Uncooked seasoned turkey suitable.
■ Microwave: Not suitable.

ABOVE LEFT: Turkey Vegetable Puffs.
ABOVE: Clockwise from top: Roast Turkey with Cashew Seasoning, Chicken with Red Peppers, Baked Liqueur Chicken.

FAMILY MAIN MEALS

Surprise is the delicious ingredient here, with a terrific mix of dishes for everyday eating and some that are a little more special for casual entertaining. There are hearty casseroles, pies and pastries, plus quick-to-make stir-fries and favorite cuts with tasty bastes and simple seasonings. Quick, too, are quail and Rock Cornish hens, unusual on the family table, but great when you want to splurge. The fastest fare would possibly be chicken marylands with honey and almonds, and Beryl's fried chicken in tasty takeout style – sure to become a family favorite!

STIR-FRIED CHICKEN AND GINGER NOODLES

1¼lb chicken thighs, boned, skinned
¼ teaspoon five-spice powder
1 clove garlic, minced
½ teaspoon Oriental sesame oil
2½ tablespoons vegetable oil
2 teaspoons grated gingerroot
1 red bell pepper, chopped
¼lb broccoli, chopped
1lb packaged fresh egg noodles
⅔ cup water
1 tablespoon dry sherry
1½ tablespoons oyster-flavored sauce
1 teaspoon cornstarch
1½ tablespoons light soy sauce
6 green onions, chopped

Cut chicken into thin strips, combine strips with spice powder, garlic and sesame oil in bowl. Heat oil in wok or large pan, add chicken strips, stir-fry until lightly browned and tender. Stir in gingerroot, pepper and broccoli, stir-fry 1 minute.

Add noodles, water, sherry, oyster sauce and blended cornstarch and soy sauce. Stir until mixture boils and thickens slightly, stir in onions.

Serves 4.

■ Best made close to serving.
■ Freeze: Not suitable.
■ Microwave: Not suitable.

CHICKEN SATAY FLAN

1 cup all-purpose flour
¼ cup (½ stick) butter
1 egg yolk
1 tablespoon lemon juice, approximately

FILLING
1½ tablespoons vegetable oil
1 onion, chopped
1 clove garlic, minced
½ teaspoon grated gingerroot
2 teaspoons curry powder
½ teaspoon ground coriander
2 cups (¾lb) finely chopped cooked chicken
¼ cup chunky peanut butter
⅓ cup canned unsweetened coconut cream
½ cup milk
1½ tablespoons light soy sauce
1 tablespoon honey
2 eggs, lightly beaten

Sift flour into bowl, rub in butter. Add egg yolk and enough juice to make ingredients cling together. Press dough into ball, knead gently on lightly floured surface until smooth, cover, refrigerate dough 30 minutes or until slightly firm.

Roll dough between sheets of baking paper until large enough to line 9 inch flan pan. Lift pastry into pan, gently ease into side, trim edge.

Place pan on baking sheet, line pastry with baking paper, fill pastry with dried beans or rice. Bake in 375°F oven 10 minutes, remove paper and beans, bake pastry further 7 minutes or until lightly browned; cool. Spoon filling into pastry case, bake in 350°F oven about 30 minutes or until set.

Filling: Heat oil in pan, add onion, garlic, gingerroot, curry powder and coriander, cook, stirring, until onion is soft; cool. Combine onion mixture with remaining ingredients in bowl; mix well.

Serves 6.

■ Flan can be made a day ahead.
■ Storage: Covered, in refrigerator.
■ Freeze: Not suitable.
■ Microwave: Filling suitable.

RIGHT: From back: Stir-Fried Chicken and Ginger Noodles, Chicken Satay Flan.

TURKEY SCHNITZELS WITH ONION THYME CREAM

**1lb boneless, skinless turkey
    breast piece**
all-purpose flour
1 egg, lightly beaten
1½ cups (3½oz) fresh bread crumbs
2½ tablespoons vegetable oil
1½ tablespoons butter

ONION THYME CREAM
2 teaspoons vegetable oil
1 onion, sliced
½ cup heavy cream
¼ cup dry white wine
**1 small chicken bouillon
    cube, crumbled**
½ teaspoon dried thyme leaves
1 teaspoon cornstarch
1 teaspoon water

Cut turkey evenly into 4 schnitzels. Toss schnitzels in flour, shake away excess flour. Dip in egg, then in bread crumbs to coat, press crumbs on firmly.

Just before serving, heat oil and butter in pan, add schnitzels, cook until browned all over and tender; drain on absorbent paper. Serve with onion thyme cream.

Onion Thyme Cream: Heat oil in pan, add onion, cook, stirring, until soft. Add cream, wine, bouillon cube and thyme. Bring to boil, simmer 1 minute. Stir in blended cornstarch and water, stir until sauce boils and thickens.

Serves 4.

■ Schnitzels can be prepared a
    day ahead.
■ Storage: Covered, in refrigerator.
■ Freeze: Uncooked schnitzels
    suitable.
■ Microwave: Sauce suitable.

ROSEMARY MUSHROOM ROCK CORNISH HENS

4 x 1lb Rock Cornish hens
2½ tablespoons vegetable oil

SEASONING
¼ cup (½ stick) butter
10 green onions, chopped
½lb slices bacon, chopped
½lb mushrooms, finely chopped
2 cups (4½oz) fresh bread crumbs
**2 tablespoons chopped
    fresh rosemary**

Fill hens with seasoning, tie legs together, tuck wings under. Brush oil over hens, place on wire rack in roasting pan. Bake in 350°F oven about 45 minutes or until well browned and cooked through.

Seasoning: Heat butter in pan, add onions and bacon, cook, stirring, until onions are soft. Add mushrooms, cook, stirring, 1 minute. Remove pan from heat, add bread crumbs and rosemary; mix well.

Serves 8.

■ Hens can be prepared a day ahead.
■ Storage: Covered, in refrigerator.
■ Freeze: Not suitable.
■ Microwave: Not suitable.

ABOVE: From top: Turkey Schnitzel with Onion Thyme Cream, Rosemary Mushroom Rock Cornish Hens.
RIGHT: Turkey with Orange Watercress Seasoning.

TURKEY WITH ORANGE WATERCRESS SEASONING

6lb self-basting turkey

ORANGE WATERCRESS SEASONING
¼ cup (½ stick) butter
1 large onion, chopped
¼lb slices bacon, chopped
2 cups (4½oz) chopped watercress
2 cups (4½oz) fresh bread crumbs
2½ tablespoons grated orange zest
⅔ cup fresh orange juice

ORANGE SAUCE
1¼ cups water
2 teaspoons grated orange zest
¾ cup fresh orange juice
1 tablespoon superfine sugar
2 small chicken bouillon cubes, crumbled
2½ tablespoons cornstarch
2½ tablespoons water, extra

Check instructions on package. Remove neck from inside turkey, wash turkey, as instructed. Fill turkey with orange watercress seasoning, secure opening with skewers, tie legs together, tuck wings under, place turkey on wire rack in roasting pan. Cover turkey with greased foil.

Bake in 325°F oven 2 hours. Remove foil, bake further 1 hour or until turkey is well browned and cooked through. Cover again with foil if browning too quickly. Drain pan, reserve 2½ tablespoons of pan juices for orange sauce. Serve turkey with orange sauce.

Orange Watercress Seasoning: Heat butter in pan, add onion and bacon, cook, stirring, until onion is soft. Combine onion mixture, watercress, bread crumbs, zest and juice in bowl; mix well.

Orange Sauce: Combine reserved pan juices, water, zest, juice, sugar and bouillon cubes in pan, bring to boil. Stir in blended cornstarch and extra water, stir until sauce boils and thickens.

Serves 6.

- Turkey best cooked close to serving.
- Freeze: Seasoned turkey suitable.
- Microwave: Seasoning and sauce suitable.

HONEY GINGER ROCK CORNISH HENS WITH CHUTNEY SAUCE

4 x 1lb Rock Cornish hens
1 teaspoon grated gingerroot
1½ tablespoons honey
2½ tablespoons vegetable oil

CORN AND PIMIENTO SEASONING
1 apple, grated
14oz can whole-kernel corn, drained
**14oz can red pimientos,
    drained, chopped**
**2½ tablespoons chopped
    fresh chives**
**1 small chicken bouillon
    cube, crumbled**
**2 cups (4½oz) fresh
    bread crumbs**
1 egg, lightly beaten
½lb ground chicken

CHUTNEY SAUCE
3 tablespoons chutney
1 teaspoon grated gingerroot
2 tablespoons light soy sauce
¾ cup water
2 teaspoons cornstarch
1½ tablespoons water, extra

Fill hens with corn and pimiento seasoning, tie legs together, tuck wings under. Place hens in lightly greased roasting pan, brush with combined gingerroot, honey and oil. Bake in 350˚F oven 20 minutes, brush again with gingerroot mixture, bake further 45 minutes or until well browned and cooked through. Cover hens with foil if beginning to brown too quickly. Serve with chutney sauce.

Corn and Pimiento Seasoning: Squeeze excess liquid from apple. Combine apple with remaining ingredients in bowl; mix well.

Chutney Sauce: Combine chutney, gingerroot, sauce and water with blended cornstarch and extra water in pan, stir over heat until sauce boils and thickens.

Serves 8.

- Hens can be prepared a day ahead.
- Storage: Covered, in refrigerator.
- Freeze: Not suitable.
- Microwave: Sauce suitable.

APRICOT TURKEY ROLL WITH FRESH HERB SEASONING

2lb oven-roasted turkey breast roll
2 teaspoons apricot jam, strained

FRESH HERB SEASONING
**1½ cups (3½oz) fresh white
    bread crumbs**
**1½ tablespoons chopped
    fresh parsley**
**1½ teaspoons caraway
    seeds, crushed**
2 teaspoons chopped fresh dill
2 teaspoons chopped fresh rosemary
1 tablespoon butter, melted
1½ tablespoons fresh orange juice
1 egg, lightly beaten

Brush turkey roll with jam. Cut deep pocket along center of roll, fill with fresh herb seasoning. Secure roll at 2 inch intervals with kitchen string. Place roll on wire rack in roasting pan, pour a little water into pan. Bake, uncovered, in 350˚F oven about 45 minutes or until lightly browned.

Fresh Herb Seasoning: Combine all ingredients in bowl; mix well.

Serves 8.

- Roll can be prepared 2 days ahead.
- Storage: Covered, in refrigerator.
- Freeze: Suitable.
- Microwave: Not suitable.

TURKEY AND EGGPLANT CASSEROLE

1 eggplant, chopped
salt
**2lb boneless, skinless turkey
    breast, chopped**
all-purpose flour
½ cup olive oil
1 onion, chopped
4 small zucchini, chopped
2 carrots, chopped
1 red bell pepper, chopped
1 green bell pepper, chopped
2 sprigs fresh rosemary
2 bay leaves
1 teaspoon dried marjoram leaves
2 cloves garlic, minced
1 cup dry red wine

Place eggplant on wire rack, sprinkle with salt, stand 20 minutes. Rinse eggplant in cold water, drain on absorbent paper.

Toss turkey in flour, shake away excess flour. Heat half the oil in pan, add turkey in batches, cook, stirring, until lightly browned; drain on absorbent paper.

Heat remaining oil in pan, add eggplant, cook, stirring, until lightly browned all over; drain on absorbent paper. Add onion, zucchini, carrots and peppers to pan, cook, stirring, until onion is soft.

Transfer vegetables and turkey to ovenproof dish (10 cup capacity). Stir in herbs, garlic and wine. Bake, covered, in 350˚F oven about 45 minutes, stirring occasionally, or until turkey is tender.

Serves 8.

- Recipe can be made a day ahead.
- Storage: Covered, in refrigerator.
- Freeze: Not suitable.
- Microwave: Not suitable.

LEFT: From top left: Turkey and Eggplant Casserole, Honey Ginger Rock Cornish Hens with Chutney Sauce, Apricot Turkey Roll with Fresh Herb Seasoning.

HEARTY CHICKEN AND BEAN CASSEROLE

½ cup dried black eye beans
1½ tablespoons vegetable oil
4 chicken marylands (thighs
　　with legs)
½lb pearl onions
1 tablespoon all-purpose flour
14½oz can tomatoes
¼ cup dry sherry
1 carrot, chopped
1 stalk celery, chopped
3oz mushrooms, chopped
2 cloves garlic, chopped
3 bay leaves
3 cloves
2 teaspoons sugar
1 small chicken bouillon
　　cube, crumbled
1 cup water

Cover beans with hot water in bowl, stand 1 hour; drain.

Heat oil in pan, add marylands, cook until well browned all over; drain on absorbent paper. Drain pan except for 1½ tablespoons pan drippings. Add onions and flour to pan, stir until well browned. Add beans, chicken, undrained crushed tomatoes and remaining ingredients; mix well. Bring to boil, simmer, covered, about 1 hour or until chicken is tender. Remove lid, boil, uncovered, further 2 minutes. Discard bay leaves and cloves before serving the casserole.

Serves 4.

■ Recipe can be made a day ahead.
■ Storage: Covered, in refrigerator.
■ Freeze: Suitable.
■ Microwave: Not suitable.

BERYL'S FRIED CHICKEN

2lb chicken pieces
1 cup all-purpose flour
2 tablespoons chicken
　　instant bouillon
½ teaspoon ground black
　　peppercorns
½ teaspoon celery salt
½ teaspoon onion salt
pinch five-spice powder
pinch garlic powder
oil for deep-frying

Do not remove skin from chicken. Add chicken to pan of boiling water, simmer, uncovered, about 5 minutes or until chicken is just cooked through; drain.

Dip chicken pieces in bowl of cold water just before tossing in combined sifted flour, instant bouillon, pepper, salts, spice powder and garlic powder. Deep-fry chicken pieces in hot oil until lightly browned and tender.

Serves 4.

■ Chicken best made close to serving.
■ Freeze: Poached chicken suitable.
■ Microwave: Not suitable.

HONEY-BRUSHED CHICKEN WITH SAVORY RICE

3lb chicken

HONEY BASTE
½ cup honey
⅓ cup light soy sauce
1 tablespoon grated gingerroot
¼ teaspoon five-spice powder

SAVORY RICE
¾ cup long-grain rice
2 tablespoons (¼ stick) butter
7oz ground pork and veal
1 small stalk celery, chopped
1 small red bell pepper, chopped
1 clove garlic, minced
6oz cooked shrimp, shelled, chopped
¼ cup canned whole-kernel
　　corn, drained
¼ cup chopped fresh parsley
2 green onions, chopped
2½ tablespoons light soy sauce

Tie legs of chicken together, tuck wings under. Place chicken on wire rack in roasting pan, brush with honey baste, cover with greased foil. Bake in 350°F oven 1 hour, brushing occasionally with baste. Remove foil, bake further 30 minutes or until skin is crisp and browned. Serve chicken with savory rice.

Honey Baste: Combine all ingredients in bowl; mix well.

Savory Rice: Add rice to pan of boiling water, boil, uncovered, about 12 minutes or until tender; drain.

Heat butter in pan, add pork and veal, celery, pepper and garlic, cook, stirring, until pork and veal are well browned. Combine rice and pork and veal mixture with remaining ingredients in bowl. Press rice mixture into 6 molds (½ cup capacity). Place molds in roasting pan, pour enough boiling water into pan to come halfway up sides of molds. Cover pan with greased foil, bake in 350°F oven 30 minutes.

Serves 6.

■ Rice molds can be prepared several hours ahead.
■ Storage: Covered, in refrigerator.
■ Freeze: Not suitable.
■ Microwave: Not suitable.

RIGHT: Clockwise from left: Hearty Chicken and Bean Casserole, Honey-Brushed Chicken with Savory Rice, Beryl's Fried Chicken.

CHICKEN, MUSHROOMS AND BACON IN RED WINE SAUCE

1½ tablespoons vegetable oil
4 chicken marylands (thighs with legs)
½lb slices bacon, chopped
8 pearl onions
2 cloves garlic, minced
1 cup dry red wine
1 cup water
1 small chicken bouillon cube, crumbled
1½ tablespoons tomato paste
¼lb button mushrooms, halved
1 tablespoon all-purpose flour
2½ tablespoons water, extra

Heat oil in pan, add chicken, cook until well browned all over; remove from pan.

Add bacon, onions and garlic to pan, cook, stirring, until bacon is browned. Stir in wine, water, bouillon cube and paste.

Return chicken to pan, bring to boil, simmer, covered, 30 minutes. Add mushrooms, simmer, uncovered, about 10 minutes or until chicken is tender. Remove chicken from pan.

Stir blended flour and extra water into pan, stir until mixture boils and thickens. Serve sauce over chicken.

Serves 4.

- Recipe can be made a day ahead.
- Storage: Covered, in refrigerator.
- Freeze: Not suitable.
- Microwave: Not suitable.

HONEY ALMOND MARYLANDS

4 chicken marylands (thighs with legs)
2 tablespoons (¼ stick) butter, melted
¼ cup honey
⅓ cup sliced almonds
1½ tablespoons light soy sauce

Place marylands in oiled roasting pan, brush with combined butter, honey, almonds and sauce. Bake in 375°F oven about 15 minutes or until well browned and tender.

Serves 4.

- Recipe best made close to serving.
- Freeze: Not suitable.
- Microwave: Not suitable.

STIR-FRIED CHICKEN CURRY

2lb chicken drumsticks
3 green onions, chopped
¼ cup light soy sauce
2½ tablespoons Chinese rice wine
2 teaspoons grated gingerroot
1 small fresh red chili
    pepper, chopped
¼ cup vegetable oil
1 large potato, chopped
1 carrot, chopped
1 onion, chopped
2½ tablespoons curry powder
¾ cup water
1 small chicken bouillon
    cube, crumbled
¼ cup Chinese rice wine, extra
2 teaspoons sugar

Cut knuckle away from thin end of each drumstick, discard knuckles. Using cleaver, cut drumsticks in half diagonally. Combine drumsticks, green onions, sauce, wine, gingerroot and chili in bowl, cover; refrigerate several hours or overnight.

Heat oil in pan, add potato, carrot and onion, cook, stirring, until lightly browned. Transfer potato mixture to bowl.

Drain drumsticks, reserve marinade. Add drumsticks to pan in single layer, cook until browned all over. Stir in curry powder, cook, stirring, 2 minutes. Stir in combined reserved marinade, water, bouillon cube, extra wine, sugar and potato mixture. Simmer, covered, about 15 minutes or until chicken is tender.

Serves 4.

■ Recipe can be made 2 days ahead.
■ Storage: Covered, in refrigerator.
■ Freeze: Not suitable.
■ Microwave: Not suitable.

LEFT: Chicken, Mushrooms and Bacon in Red Wine Sauce.
ABOVE: From left: Honey Almond Maryland, Stir-Fried Chicken Curry.

MINTED MARYLANDS WITH NUTTY HERB SEASONING

**4 chicken marylands (thighs
   with legs)**
2½ tablespoons mint jelly
1 tablespoon chopped fresh mint
**1½ tablespoons chopped
   fresh parsley**
⅓ cup packaged ground hazelnuts
⅓ cup fresh bread crumbs
1½ tablespoons butter, melted
⅓ cup grated fresh Parmesan cheese

Make a pocket in each maryland by sliding fingers gently between skin and meat. Combine jelly, herbs, nuts and bread crumbs in bowl. Push mixture evenly under skin, secure openings with small skewers or toothpicks. Place chicken in greased roasting pan, brush with butter, bake, uncovered, in 350°F oven 20 minutes. Sprinkle with cheese, bake further 20 minutes or until chicken is well browned and tender.

   Serves 4.

- Chicken can be prepared a
   day ahead.
- Storage: Covered, in refrigerator.
- Freeze: Not suitable.
- Microwave: Not suitable.

APRICOT AND CHICKEN RICE SALAD

1½ cups (10oz) long-grain white rice
1½ tablespoons vegetable oil
2 tablespoons (¼ stick) butter
**2 boneless, skinless chicken
   breast halves**
¼ cup slivered almonds, toasted
¼ cup pine nuts, toasted
3½oz dried apricots, sliced
1 tablespoon chopped fresh cilantro
½ cup pitted black olives
4 green onions, chopped
¼ cup shredded coconut
½ cup apricot nectar

Add rice to large pan of boiling water, boil, uncovered, about 12 minutes or until tender; drain. Rinse rice under cold water; drain well.

   Heat oil and butter in pan, add chicken, cook until well browned all over and tender; cool.

   Slice chicken. Combine rice, chicken, nuts, apricots, cilantro, olives, onions and coconut in bowl.

Just before serving, add nectar to salad; toss well.

   Serves 4.

- Salad can be made a day ahead.
- Storage: Covered, in refrigerator.
- Freeze: Not suitable.
- Microwave: Rice suitable.

TRADITIONAL ROAST TURKEY WITH BROWN GRAVY

6lb turkey
2½ tablespoons vegetable oil
2½ tablespoons all-purpose flour
**1 large chicken bouillon
   cube, crumbled**
2 cups water

BACON SEASONING
2 tablespoons (¼ stick) butter
6oz slices bacon, chopped
1 onion, chopped
2 stalks celery, chopped
**7oz packaged seasoned
   stuffing mix**
1 cup (2½oz) fresh bread crumbs
2 eggs, lightly beaten
¼ cup water
½ teaspoon dried mixed herbs

Remove neck from inside turkey, wash turkey well, pat dry inside and out. Fill turkey with bacon seasoning, secure opening with skewers. Tie legs together, tuck wings under, place turkey on wire rack in roasting pan, add a little water to pan. Brush oil evenly over turkey.

   Bake in 350°F oven about 2½ hours or until turkey is well browned and tender, brushing with pan drippings every 20 minutes. Cover legs, wings and breast with foil during cooking if turkey is browning too quickly.

   Drain all but 1½ tablespoons pan drippings from pan. Place pan over heat, add flour, cook, stirring, until mixture is lightly browned. Remove from heat, gradually stir in combined bouillon cube and the 2 cups water. Stir over heat until gravy boils, simmer, uncovered, until thickened; strain. Serve turkey with gravy.

Bacon Seasoning: Heat butter in pan, add bacon, onion and celery, cook, stirring, until onion is soft. Combine stuffing mix, bread crumbs, eggs, water and herbs in bowl; mix well. Add bacon mixture to bowl; mix well.

   Serves 6.

- Turkey can be prepared a day
   ahead. Gravy best made just
   before serving.
- Storage: Covered, in refrigerator.
- Freeze: Uncooked seasoned
   turkey suitable.
- Microwave: Suitable.

LEFT: Clockwise from top: Traditional Roast Turkey with Brown Gravy, Apricot and Chicken Rice Salad, Minted Marylands with Nutty Herb Seasoning.

FRUITY CHICKEN PASTRIES

1 apple, grated
1 carrot, grated
2 cups (10oz) chopped
    cooked chicken
½ cup cottage cheese
½ cup golden raisins
¼ teaspoon ground cinnamon
8 sheets phyllo pastry
3oz cup (¾ stick) butter, melted

Squeeze excess liquid from apple and carrot. Combine in bowl with chicken, cheese, raisins and cinnamon.

Layer 2 sheets of pastry together, brushing each with butter. Fold pastry in half, place quarter of the chicken mixture in center of pastry, fold in sides and fold over to form a parcel. Repeat with remaining pastry, butter and chicken mixture. Place pastries on lightly greased baking sheet, brush with butter.

Just before serving, bake pastries in 375°F oven about 15 minutes or until well browned and heated through.

Serves 4.

- ■ Recipe can be prepared a day ahead.
- ■ Storage: Covered, in refrigerator.
- ■ Freeze: Not suitable.
- ■ Microwave: Not suitable.

GOLDEN CHICKEN MARYLANDS

4 chicken marylands (thighs
    with legs)
2 bananas, halved
15oz can pineapple slices, drained
all-purpose flour
2 eggs, lightly beaten
½ cup milk
2 cups (7oz) packaged unseasoned
    bread crumbs
oil for deep-frying

Toss marylands, bananas and pineapple slices in flour; shake away excess flour. Dip in combined eggs and milk, then in bread crumbs to coat.

Just before serving, deep-fry marylands in hot oil about 10 minutes or until lightly browned and cooked through, drain on absorbent paper; keep warm. Deep-fry bananas and pineapple in hot oil until lightly browned; drain on absorbent paper.

Serves 4.

- ■ Marylands can be prepared a day ahead. Fruit best prepared just before serving.
- ■ Storage: Covered, in refrigerator.
- ■ Freeze: Crumbed chicken suitable.
- ■ Microwave: Not suitable.

PINEAPPLE PEPPER CHICKEN

1½ tablespoons vegetable oil
8 chicken thigh cutlets
2 tablespoons (¼ stick) butter
1 teaspoon grated gingerroot
½ small pineapple, chopped
1 red bell pepper, sliced
1 teaspoon cornstarch
¼ cup water
2 tablespoons dark brown sugar

Heat oil in pan, add chicken, cook until chicken is well browned and tender. Remove chicken from pan; drain on absorbent paper.

Heat butter in same pan, add gingerroot, pineapple and pepper, cook, stirring, 1 minute. Stir in blended cornstarch, water and sugar, cook, stirring, until mixture boils and thickens. Return chicken to pan, stir until heated through.

Serves 4.

- ■ Best made close to serving.
- ■ Freeze: Suitable.
- ■ Microwave: Suitable.

ABOVE: Pineapple Pepper Chicken.
RIGHT: Clockwise from top: Spring Chicken and Pasta Salad, Fruity Chicken Pastries, Golden Chicken Maryland.

SPRING CHICKEN AND PASTA SALAD

2 cups (5½oz) pasta twists
1 carrot
1 red bell pepper
2 zucchini, sliced
2 cups (10oz) chopped
   cooked chicken
14oz can whole-kernel corn, drained
2 green onions, chopped

DRESSING
¼ cup sour cream
¼ cup mayonnaise
½ cup Italian salad dressing

Add pasta to large pan of boiling water, boil, uncovered, until just tender; drain. Rinse pasta under cold water; drain well.
   Cut carrot and pepper into thin strips. Combine pasta, carrot and pepper in bowl with remaining ingredients.

Just before serving, pour over dressing; toss well.
Dressing: Combine cream and mayonnaise in bowl; whisk in salad dressing.

   Serves 4.

- Salad can be prepared 3 hours ahead.
- Storage: Covered, in refrigerator.
- Freeze: Not suitable.
- Microwave: Pasta suitable.

CHEESY POTATO AND CHICKEN FLAN

¾lb potatoes
3 eggs, lightly beaten
1½ tablespoons chopped
    fresh parsley
1½ tablespoons chopped fresh basil
1 tablespoon chopped fresh chives
1 cup (¼lb) grated cheddar cheese

FILLING
2 cups (10oz) chopped
    cooked chicken
2½ tablespoons mayonnaise
1½ tablespoons tomato paste
⅔ cup heavy cream

Line base and side of 8 inch springform pan with foil; grease foil. Add whole potatoes to pan of boiling water, simmer, uncovered, about 5 minutes or until partially cooked. Drain, rinse under cold water, drain well; cool.

Coarsely grate potatoes into bowl; stir in eggs, herbs and half the cheese. Press half the mixture evenly over base of prepared pan, spread evenly with filling, top evenly with remaining potato mixture. Smooth surface, sprinkle with remaining cheese. Bake in 350°F oven about 1 hour or until firm. Stand flan 10 minutes before cutting. Serve hot or cold.

Filling: Blend or process all ingredients until smooth.

Serves 6.

■ Recipe can be made a day ahead.
■ Storage: Covered, in refrigerator.
■ Freeze: Not suitable.
■ Microwave: Not suitable.

CHICKEN DRUMMETTES IN GINGER PLUM SAUCE

2½ tablespoons vegetable oil
2lb chicken drummettes
1 clove garlic, minced
1½ tablespoons grated gingerroot
3 green onions, chopped
⅔ cup plum sauce
1½ tablespoons light soy sauce
1½ tablespoons cornstarch
¼ cup water

Heat oil in pan, add drummettes, cook about 15 minutes, or until lightly browned all over and cooked through. Drain excess oil from pan, add garlic, gingerroot, onions, sauces and blended cornstarch and water to drummettes in pan. Stir until mixture boils and thickens, simmer, uncovered, 10 minutes.

Serves 4.

■ Recipe can be made a day ahead.
■ Storage: Covered, in refrigerator.
■ Freeze: Suitable.
■ Microwave: Not suitable.

CHICKEN SCHNITZELS WITH LEMON CHIVE SAUCE

4 boneless, skinless chicken
    breast halves
all-purpose flour
2 eggs, lightly beaten
2½ tablespoons milk
packaged unseasoned bread crumbs
⅓ cup vegetable oil

LEMON CHIVE SAUCE
1 tablespoon cornstarch
1 cup water
¼ cup lemon juice
1 small chicken bouillon
    cube, crumbled
1 tablespoon honey
1 tablespoon dark brown sugar
1½ tablespoons chopped
    fresh chives

Using meat mallet, gently pound chicken between plastic wrap until thin. Toss schnitzels in flour, shake away excess flour. Dip into combined eggs and milk, then in bread crumbs to coat.

Just before serving, heat oil in pan, add schnitzels, cook until well browned and tender. Serve with lemon chive sauce.

Lemon Chive Sauce: Blend cornstarch with water in pan, add juice, bouillon cube, honey and sugar. Stir over heat until sauce boils and thickens. Stir in chives.

Serves 4.

■ Schnitzels can be prepared 2 days ahead. Sauce best made just before serving.
■ Storage: Covered, in refrigerator.
■ Freeze: Uncooked schnitzels suitable.
■ Microwave: Sauce suitable.

RIGHT: Clockwise from left: Chicken Schnitzels with Lemon Chive Sauce, Chicken Drummettes in Ginger Plum Sauce, Cheesy Potato and Chicken Flan.

CHUNKY CHICKEN PIE WITH CHEESE TOPPING

¾ cup brown rice
1½ tablespoons butter
1 tablespoon vegetable oil
1 onion, sliced
1 red bell pepper, sliced
1 clove garlic, sliced
3 small zucchini, sliced
2 cups (10oz) chopped
   cooked chicken
¾ cup grated cheddar cheese

CHEESE SAUCE
2½ tablespoons butter
2½ tablespoons all-purpose flour
1½ cups milk
¾ cup grated cheddar cheese

Lightly grease ovenproof dish (8 cup capacity). Add rice to large pan of boiling water, boil, uncovered, about 30 minutes or until tender; drain.

Heat butter and oil in pan, add onion, pepper and garlic, cook, stirring, until onion is soft. Add zucchini, cook, stirring, 1 minute. Combine vegetable mixture, rice, chicken and cheese sauce in bowl, spoon into prepared dish. Sprinkle with cheese, bake in 350°F oven about 30 minutes or until well browned.

Cheese Sauce: Heat butter in pan, add flour, cook, stirring, 1 minute, remove from heat. Gradually stir in milk, stir over heat until sauce boils and thickens. Remove from heat, add cheese, stir until melted.

Serves 4 to 6.

- Recipe can be prepared a day ahead.
- Storage: Covered, in refrigerator.
- Freeze: Cooked pie suitable.
- Microwave: Cheese sauce suitable.

HONEY SESAME CHICKEN IN LIGHT BATTER

1¼lb chicken thighs, boned, skinned
¼ teaspoon five-spice powder
¼ teaspoon Oriental sesame oil
cornstarch
oil for deep-frying
1 tablespoon vegetable oil, extra
2½ tablespoons honey
2½ tablespoons sesame seeds

BATTER
¾ cup self-rising flour
¼ cup cornstarch
1¼ cups water
1 egg, lightly beaten

Cut chicken into chunky strips, combine with spice powder and sesame oil in bowl, cover, stand 10 minutes.

Toss chicken in cornstarch, shake away excess cornstarch. Dip chicken in batter to coat evenly. Deep-fry chicken in hot oil until well browned and cooked through; drain on absorbent paper.

Heat extra oil in pan, add honey, stir until heated through. Add chicken, toss well; sprinkle with sesame seeds.

Batter: Sift flours into bowl, gradually stir in combined water and egg; mix to a smooth thin batter.

Serves 4.

- Best made close to serving.
- Freeze: Not suitable.
- Microwave: Not suitable.

CHICKEN AND RICE PILAU

2lb chicken
8 cups cold water
4 cardamom pods, bruised
10 black peppercorns
1 clove
1 onion, chopped
2½ cups (1lb) long-grain rice
4 saffron threads
2 teaspoons hot water
½ cup (1 stick) butter
1 onion, chopped, extra
1 clove garlic, minced
½ teaspoon grated gingerroot
½ teaspoon grated orange zest
½ teaspoon garam masala
½ teaspoon ground cardamom
1 tablespoon orange flower water
¼ cup golden raisins

Combine chicken, cold water, cardamom pods, peppercorns, clove and onion in large pan, bring to boil, simmer, uncovered, about 1 hour or until liquid is reduced to about 5 cups.

Remove chicken from pan, strain broth into large bowl, discard spices and onion.

Remove skin from chicken, remove meat from bones, discard skin and bones. Cut meat into thin strips, cover, refrigerate until ready to use.

Cool broth, cover, refrigerate overnight. Cover rice with water in bowl, stand 30 minutes; drain. Combine saffron and the hot water in small bowl, stand 10 minutes. Skim fat from broth, reserve broth.

Heat butter in large pan, add extra onion, cook, stirring, until onion is soft. Stir in garlic, gingerroot, zest, garam masala, ground cardamom, orange flower water and saffron mixture, cook, stirring, until garlic is lightly browned. Stir in reserved broth, rice and raisins, bring to boil, simmer, covered, about 10 minutes or until all liquid is absorbed and rice is tender. Stir in reserved chicken meat.

Serves 8.

- Best made close to serving.
- Storage: Covered, in refrigerator.
- Freeze: Not suitable.
- Microwave: Not suitable.

LEFT: Chunky Chicken Pie with Cheese Topping.
RIGHT: From top: Honey Sesame Chicken in Light Batter, Chicken and Rice Pilau.

QUICK FRIED RICE WITH CHICKEN

¾lb chicken thighs, boned, skinned
½ cup water
1 small chicken bouillon
    cube, crumbled
1½ tablespoons vegetable oil
1 egg, lightly beaten
1 clove garlic, minced
1 teaspoon grated gingerroot
3 green onions, chopped
¼lb slices bacon, chopped
1 red bell pepper, chopped
½ cup canned drained sliced
    bamboo shoots
½ cup frozen green peas
2½ tablespoons light soy sauce
3 cups cooked rice

Combine chicken, water and bouillon cube in pan, bring to boil, simmer, covered, about 6 minutes or until chicken is tender. Drain chicken, cut into thin strips.

Heat oil in large wok or pan, add egg, cook until set, turn egg, cook on other side until lightly browned, remove from pan, cut into thin strips.

Add garlic, gingerroot, onions, bacon, pepper, bamboo shoots and peas to pan, stir-fry over heat until bacon is cooked. Stir in chicken strips, egg strips, sauce and cooked rice, stir-fry until heated through.

Serves 4 to 6.

■ Recipe can be made a day ahead.
■ Storage: Covered, in refrigerator.
■ Freeze: Suitable.
■ Microwave: Not suitable.

LIGHT 'N' EASY BUTTERED ROCK CORNISH HENS

2½ tablespoons lemon juice
2 x 1lb Rock Cornish hens, halved
¼ cup (½ stick) butter, melted
1 teaspoon French mustard
1 teaspoon paprika
2 teaspoons chopped fresh tarragon

Sprinkle juice over hens. Combine butter, mustard, paprika and tarragon; mix well. Broil hens until tender, brush with butter mixture during cooking.

Serves 2 to 4.

■ Recipe best made just before serving.
■ Freeze: Not suitable.
■ Microwave: Not suitable.

CREAMY CHICKEN AND POTATO BAKE

2lb potatoes, finely sliced
1 onion, sliced
2½ cups (¾lb) chopped
    cooked chicken
½ cup grated cheddar cheese
½ teaspoon cracked black
    peppercorns
1½ tablespoons chopped
    fresh chives
1¼ cups heavy cream
½ teaspoon paprika

Lightly grease shallow ovenproof dish (6 cup capacity). Place half the potato over base of prepared dish, top with onion, chicken, cheese, peppercorns and chives. Pour over half the cream. Top with remaining potato, remaining cream, sprinkle with paprika. Bake in 350˚F oven about 1½ hours or until browned and potato is tender.

Serves 4.

■ Recipe best made just before serving.
■ Freeze: Not suitable.
■ Microwave: Not suitable.

RIGHT: Clockwise from top: Creamy Chicken and Potato Bake, Light 'n' Easy Buttered Rock Cornish Hens, Quick Fried Rice with Chicken.

QUICK CURRIED CHICKEN AND BROCCOLI

**3 cups (15oz) chopped
  cooked chicken
6oz broccoli, chopped
14½oz can condensed creamy
  chicken soup
2 teaspoons curry powder
2½ tablespoons lemon juice
½ cup mayonnaise
¾ cup grated cheddar cheese
½ cup packaged unseasoned
  bread crumbs**

Lightly grease ovenproof dish (6 cup capacity). Spread chicken into dish. Boil, steam or microwave broccoli until just soft, rinse under cold water; drain. Place broccoli over chicken. Combine undiluted soup, curry powder, juice and mayonnaise in pan. Bring to boil, pour over chicken and broccoli. Sprinkle with combined cheese and bread crumbs, bake, uncovered, in 350°F oven about 10 minutes or until cheese is melted.

Serves 4.

- Recipe best made just before serving.
- Freeze: Suitable.
- Microwave: Suitable.

CHICKEN AND BACON ROLLS WITH PARSLEY DRESSING

**8 chicken thighs, boned, skinned
2 teaspoons seeded mustard
8 thick slices bacon**

PARSLEY DRESSING
**2½ tablespoons pine nuts, toasted
2 cups fresh parsley sprigs
2 cloves garlic, minced
½ cup olive oil
2½ tablespoons grated fresh
  Parmesan cheese**

Spread chicken with mustard, roll up. Wrap a bacon slice around each roll, secure with toothpicks. Broil rolls about 10 minutes or until cooked through. Remove toothpicks, serve with parsley dressing.
Parsley Dressing: Blend or process nuts, parsley, garlic and half the oil until smooth. With motor operating, gradually pour in remaining oil in a thin stream. Stir in cheese; mix well

Serves 4.

- Rolls can be prepared 2 days ahead. Dressing best made just before serving.
- Storage: Covered, in refrigerator.
- Freeze: Uncooked rolls suitable.
- Microwave: Suitable.

*LEFT: From top: Quick Curried Chicken and Broccoli, Chicken and Bacon Rolls with Parsley Dressing.
RIGHT: Braised Chicken with Cabbage.*

BRAISED CHICKEN WITH CABBAGE

**¼ cup vegetable oil
1 leek, chopped
1 red onion, sliced
½ small cabbage, shredded
14½oz can tomatoes
1½ tablespoons balsamic vinegar
1 cup water
1 small chicken bouillon
  cube, crumbled
8 chicken thighs, boned, skinned
all-purpose flour
1 tablespoon chopped fresh parsley**

Heat 1 tablespoon of the oil in pan, add leek and onion, cook, stirring, until leek is soft. Stir in cabbage, cook, covered, until just soft. Stir in undrained crushed tomatoes, vinegar and combined water and bouillon cube. Bring to boil, simmer, uncovered, about 10 minutes or until liquid is reduced by half. Transfer mixture to ovenproof dish (12 cup capacity).

Toss chicken in flour, shake away excess flour. Heat remaining oil in pan, add chicken, cook until lightly browned all over. Place chicken over cabbage in dish. Bake, covered, in 350°F oven about 45 minutes or until chicken is tender. Sprinkle with parsley before serving.

Serves 4.

- Best made just before serving.
- Freeze: Not suitable.
- Microwave: Not suitable.

DRUMSTICKS FLORENTINE

**10oz package chopped frozen
    spinach, thawed**
8 chicken drumsticks
½ cup grated cheddar cheese
¼ teaspoon ground nutmeg
2 teaspoons Worcestershire sauce

Squeeze excess liquid from spinach. Loosen skin on 1 side of each drumstick by sliding a finger carefully between skin and meat. Combine spinach, cheese and nutmeg in bowl, push mixture into pockets, secure openings with toothpicks.
Just before serving, place drumsticks in oiled ovenproof dish, brush with sauce. Bake, uncovered, in 375°F oven about 40 minutes or until well browned and tender.

Serves 4.

■ Chicken can be prepared a
    day ahead.
■ Storage: Covered, in refrigerator.
■ Freeze: Suitable.
■ Microwave: Suitable.

SWEET AND SOUR STIR-FRIED CHICKEN

2½ tablespoons vegetable oil
**2lb chicken thighs, boned,
    skinned, sliced**
7oz can pineapple chunks
2 teaspoons light soy sauce
2½ tablespoons tomato ketchup
1½ tablespoons sugar
1½ tablespoons brown vinegar
1½ tablespoons lemon juice
1 teaspoon grated gingerroot
1½ tablespoons cornstarch
¾ cup water
1 red bell pepper, chopped
2 stalks celery, chopped
2 green onions, chopped
10oz can mandarin segments, drained

Heat oil in large wok or pan, add chicken in batches, stir-fry until lightly browned and cooked through, drain on absorbent paper; keep warm.

Drain pineapple, reserve syrup. Drain excess oil from wok. Add reserved syrup, sauce, ketchup, sugar, vinegar, juice and gingerroot with blended cornstarch and water to wok. Stir over heat until mixture boils and thickens. Add pineapple, pepper and celery, cook 1 minute. Add chicken, green onions and mandarins, stir until heated through.

Serves 6.

■ Best made just before serving.
■ Freeze: Not suitable.
■ Microwave: Not suitable.

MUSTARD CHICKEN PIE

1½ cups all-purpose flour
¼ cup (½ stick) butter
⅓ cup sour cream
1 egg, lightly beaten

FILLING
2 tablespoons (¼ stick) butter
1 clove garlic, minced
2 leeks, chopped
1 carrot, chopped
2½ tablespoons seeded mustard
2 teaspoons chopped fresh thyme
**2lb chicken thighs, boned,
    skinned, chopped**
1 cup (¼lb) fresh or frozen peas
½ cup sour cream
1½ tablespoons cornstarch
2½ tablespoons water

Sift flour into bowl, rub in butter, add cream, mix to a firm ball. Knead lightly on floured surface until smooth. (Or, make by processor.) Cover, refrigerate 30 minutes.

Spoon filling into 8 inch pie plate. Roll pastry on lightly floured surface until large enough to cover top of plate, place over filling, pinch edge. Brush pastry with egg, cut a slit in pastry, decorate with pastry leaves, if desired. Bake chicken pie in 350°F oven about 45 minutes or until pastry is browned.

Filling: Melt butter in pan, add garlic, cook, stirring, 1 minute. Stir in leeks, carrot, mustard and thyme, cook, stirring, 2 minutes. Add chicken, cook about 10 minutes, stirring occasionally, or until chicken is tender. Stir in peas and cream, then blended cornstarch and water, stir until mixture boils and thickens; cool.

Serves 6.

■ Pie can be prepared a day ahead.
■ Storage: Covered, in refrigerator.
■ Freeze: Not suitable.
■ Microwave: Filling suitable.

LEFT: Clockwise from top: Mustard Chicken Pie, Drumsticks Florentine, Sweet and Sour Stir-Fried Chicken.

CRUSTY CHICKEN CASSEROLE WITH CHEESE BATTER

1 onion, chopped
2 green onions, chopped
1 stalk celery, chopped
¼ cup water
2 tablespoons (¼ stick) butter
6oz slices bacon, chopped
2oz mushrooms, sliced
14½oz can condensed creamy
   chicken soup
½ cup sour cream
3 cups (15oz) chopped
   cooked chicken
¼ cup grated cheddar cheese

CHEESE BATTER
1 cup self-rising flour
1 small red bell pepper, chopped
1 small green bell pepper, chopped
2 eggs, lightly beaten
1 cup (¼lb) grated cheddar cheese
½ cup milk

Combine onion, green onions, celery and water in pan, simmer, covered, until onion is soft. Heat butter in pan, add bacon and mushrooms, cook, stirring, 3 minutes. Combine onion mixture, undiluted soup, sour cream, chicken and bacon mixture in bowl. Pour mixture into greased ovenproof dish (8 cup capacity).

Just before serving, spread cheese batter over chicken mixture. Bake in 350°F oven about 40 minutes or until lightly browned and firm. Sprinkle with cheese, return to oven, bake further 5 minutes or until cheese is melted.

Cheese Batter: Sift flour into bowl, add peppers, eggs, cheese and milk, stir until just combined.

Serves 6.

- Casserole, without batter, can be prepared 2 days ahead.
- Storage: Covered, in refrigerator.
- Freeze: Not suitable.
- Microwave: Not suitable.

PIMIENTO RICE CHICKEN WITH PIMIENTO SAUCE

1½ tablespoons vegetable oil
1 onion, chopped
2 cloves garlic, chopped
1 chorizo sausage, chopped
6 pitted black olives, finely chopped
1 cup cooked rice
13oz can pimientos, drained, chopped
3lb chicken

PIMIENTO SAUCE
10oz can Tomato Supreme
1½ tablespoons tomato paste
¼ cup water
4 green onions, chopped

Heat half the oil in pan, add onion and garlic, cook, stirring, until onion is soft. Combine onion mixture, sausage, olives, rice and half the pimientos; reserve remaining pimientos for sauce.

Spoon onion mixture into chicken, secure opening with skewer, tie legs together, tuck wings under. Rub chicken with remaining oil. Place chicken in lightly greased roasting pan. Bake in 350°F oven about 1¼ hours or until well browned and tender. Serve with pimiento sauce.

Pimiento Sauce: Blend or process reserved pimientos, Tomato Supreme, paste and water until smooth. Combine in pan with onions, stir until heated through.

Serves 4 to 6.

- Recipe best made just before serving.
- Freeze: Seasoned chicken suitable.
- Microwave: Sauce suitable.

FRUITY CHICKEN RISOTTO

2½ tablespoons olive oil
1 onion, chopped
7oz button mushrooms, halved
¼lb slices bacon, chopped
1 cup long-grain rice
2 small chicken bouillon
   cubes, crumbled
2⅓ cups water
1½ tablespoons light soy sauce
2 cups (10oz) chopped
   cooked chicken
¼ cup chopped unsalted
   roasted cashews
⅓ cup thinly sliced dried apricots
3½ oz fresh dates, pitted, chopped
1 green onion, chopped
2½ tablespoons chopped
   fresh parsley

Heat oil in pan, add onion, mushrooms and bacon, cook, stirring occasionally, 10 minutes. Add rice, cook, stirring, 5 minutes. Stir in combined bouillon cubes, water and sauce. Bring to boil, simmer, covered, about 20 minutes or until all liquid is absorbed and rice is tender. Stir in chicken, cashews, apricots, dates, green onion and parsley. Stand, covered, 5 minutes before serving.

Serves 6.

- Best made just before serving.
- Freeze: Not suitable.
- Microwave: Suitable.

RIGHT: Clockwise from left: Crusty Chicken Casserole with Cheese Batter, Fruity Chicken Risotto, Pimiento Rice Chicken with Pimiento Sauce.

CHICKEN LOAVES WITH CREAMY PEPPERCORN SAUCE

1lb ground chicken
½ cup fresh bread crumbs
¼ cup cooked rice
2 teaspoons seeded mustard
4 thick slices bacon
2 green onions

CREAMY PEPPERCORN SAUCE
2 teaspoons butter
1 green onion, chopped
2 teaspoons canned drained green
    peppercorns, crushed
½ small chicken bouillon
    cube, crumbled
¾ cup heavy cream
¼ cup milk
1½ teaspoons cornstarch
2 teaspoons water

Lightly grease 4 x 2 inch x 3½ inch mini loaf pans. Combine chicken, bread crumbs, rice and mustard in bowl. Halve bacon crossways. Line base and sides of prepared pans with bacon, allowing bacon to overlap edges of pans.

Spread half the chicken mixture evenly into pans. Cut onions into 3½ inch lengths, place over chicken. Spread evenly with remaining chicken mixture, fold over bacon; press lightly.

Place pans on baking sheet, bake in 350°F oven about 40 minutes or until loaves are firm. Stand 5 minutes, turn onto absorbent paper. Serve sliced with creamy peppercorn sauce and fettuccine tossed in butter and poppy seeds.

Creamy Peppercorn Sauce: Heat butter in pan, add onion and peppercorns, cook, stirring, until onion is soft. Stir in combined bouillon cube, cream and milk. Bring to boil, simmer, uncovered, 2 minutes. Stir in blended cornstarch and water, stir until sauce boils and thickens.

Serves 4.

■ Loaves can be made a day ahead.
■ Storage: Covered, in refrigerator.
■ Freeze: Loaves suitable.
■ Microwave: Sauce suitable.

BUTTERFLIED CHICKEN WITH FRESH HERB SEASONING

3lb chicken
1 teaspoon vegetable oil
1 clove garlic, minced

FRESH HERB SEASONING
¼ cup (½ stick) butter
1 large onion, finely chopped
1 red bell pepper, finely chopped
1½ tablespoons chopped
    fresh rosemary
¼ cup chopped fresh cilantro
3 cups (7oz) fresh bread crumbs

Using sharp knife or scissors, cut along either side of backbone, remove and discard backbone. Place chicken, breast-side-up on bench, flatten with hand or rolling pin. Loosen skin over breast and

CHICKEN AND LYCHEES STIR-FRY

1lb boneless, skinless chicken
    breasts, thinly sliced
cornstarch
oil for deep-frying
1 tablespoon vegetable oil, extra
1 small fresh red chili pepper,
    finely chopped
5 green onions, chopped
1 green bell pepper, chopped
¾ cup water
½ cup tomato ketchup
1 tablespoon dark brown sugar
2 teaspoons cornstarch, extra
2½ tablespoons water, extra
1lb fresh lychees, peeled

Toss chicken in cornstarch, shake away excess cornstarch. Deep-fry chicken in hot oil until lightly browned and tender; drain on absorbent paper.

Just before serving, heat extra oil in wok or pan, add chili, green onions and pepper, stir-fry until pepper is soft. Stir in combined water, ketchup and sugar, bring to boil, simmer, uncovered, 5 minutes. Stir in blended extra cornstarch and extra water with lychees and chicken, stir over heat until mixture boils and thickens.

Serves 4.

■ Recipe best made close to serving.
■ Freeze: Not suitable.
■ Microwave: Not suitable.

drumsticks by sliding fingers between skin and meat. Push seasoning evenly under skin. Place chicken in roasting pan, rub with combined oil and garlic. Bake, uncovered, in 350°F oven about 1½ hours or until chicken is browned and tender, stand 15 minutes before serving.

Fresh Herb Seasoning: Heat butter in pan, add onion and pepper, cook, stirring, until onion is soft. Stir in herbs and bread crumbs; mix well.

Serves 6.

- ■ Chicken can be prepared 2 days ahead.
- ■ Storage: Covered, in refrigerator.
- ■ Freeze: Seasoned chicken suitable.
- ■ Microwave: Not suitable.

MUSTARD MARYLANDS

4 chicken marylands (thighs with legs)
¼ cup mayonnaise

MUSTARD HOLLANDAISE
3 egg yolks
2½ tablespoons lemon juice
½ cup (1 stick) butter, melted
1 tablespoon seeded mustard

Place marylands in greased roasting pan, brush with mayonnaise, bake in 350°F oven about 45 minutes or until tender. Serve with mustard hollandaise.

Mustard Hollandaise: Blend or process egg yolks and juice. Gradually pour in hot bubbling butter while motor is operating. Blend until thick, stir in mustard.

Serves 4.

- ■ Best made close to serving.
- ■ Freeze: Not suitable.
- ■ Microwave: Not suitable.

ABOVE LEFT: From top: Chicken Loaves with Creamy Peppercorn Sauce, Chicken and Lychees Stir-Fry.
ABOVE: From top: Butterflied Chicken with Fresh Herb Seasoning, Mustard Marylands.

ELEGANT LUNCHES

We're really putting chic into chicken with our super smart recipes; some are super easy, too! But there is more than chicken, of course, in salads of subtle flair, or lovingly encased in pastry. There's also the hot and hearty, such as glazed turkey buffe with bacon muffins, or the cassoulet of quail. When you have extra time, follow our pictures to the unusual pastry in mushroom chicken tartlets, or make smoked chicken de luxe. When time is short, present bought smoked turkey with a luscious mayonnaise or think of sweet chili duck on bagels.

CASSOULET OF QUAIL WITH THYME AND LENTILS

1 cup brown lentils
8 quail
all-purpose flour
¼ cup olive oil
¼ cup (½ stick) butter
¼ cup (½ stick) butter, extra
1 onion, chopped
2 teaspoons chopped fresh thyme
1 clove garlic, minced
½lb slices bacon, chopped
**1 teaspoon cracked black
    peppercorns**
4 cups water
**2 large chicken bouillon
    cubes, crumbled**
½ cup dry red wine

Cover lentils with water in bowl, stand for 30 minutes; drain well. Cut quail in half, toss in flour, shake away excess flour.

Heat oil and butter in pan, add quail, cook until well browned all over, remove quail. Add extra butter to pan, add onion, thyme, garlic and bacon, cook, stirring, until onion is soft. Stir in lentils, cook further 2 minutes. Stir in peppercorns, water, bouillon cubes and wine, bring to boil, simmer, covered, 5 minutes. Simmer, uncovered, further 20 minutes or until lentils are tender.

Add quail, simmer, uncovered, further 10 minutes or until quail are tender and lentil mixture is thick. Serve sprinkled with extra thyme, if desired.

Serves 8.
- Recipe best made just before serving.
- Freeze: Suitable.
- Microwave: Not suitable.

SESAME CHICKEN AND MANDARIN SALAD

1¼lb chicken thighs, boned, skinned
1 tablespoon vegetable oil
¼lb snow peas
¼lb yellow pattypan squash, sliced
¼lb mushrooms, sliced
1 red bell pepper, sliced
¼lb mung bean sprouts
**10oz can mandarin
    segments, drained**
**¾ cup canned sliced water
    chestnuts, drained**
**2½ tablespoons sesame
    seeds, toasted**
1 lollo rosso lettuce

SESAME DRESSING
1½ tablespoons Oriental sesame oil
2 teaspoons vegetable oil
2½ tablespoons lemon juice
1 teaspoon superfine sugar
1 clove garlic, minced

Cut chicken into strips. Heat oil in pan, add chicken, cook, stirring, until chicken is lightly browned and tender, drain; cool.

Boil steam or microwave peas and squash until just tender; drain. Rinse under cold water; drain.

Combine chicken, peas, squash, mushrooms, pepper, sprouts, mandarin segments, water chestnuts and seeds in bowl. Add sesame dressing; toss well. Serve over lettuce.

Sesame Dressing: Combine all ingredients in bowl; mix well.

Serves 4.
- Salad can be prepared a day ahead.
- Storage: Covered, in refrigerator.
- Freeze: Not suitable.
- Microwave: Vegetables suitable.

RIGHT: From left: Sesame Chicken and Mandarin Salad, Cassoulet of Quail with Thyme and Lentils.

TURKEY WALDORF RING

1 cup (4oz) small pasta shells
15 slices smoked turkey
2 stalks celery, chopped
1 small red bell pepper, chopped
1 small apple, chopped
4 green onions, chopped
⅓ cup golden raisins
⅓ cup chopped pecans
1½ tablespoons unflavored gelatin
2½ tablespoons water
¾ cup sour cream
¾ cup mayonnaise
½ cup heavy cream

Line base and side of 8 inch tube pan with paper. Add pasta to large pan of boiling water, boil, uncovered, until just tender, drain; cool.

Line base of prepared pan evenly with 9 slices of turkey, cut remaining slices in half, use to line sides of pan.

Combine pasta, celery, pepper, apple, onions, raisins and nuts in bowl. Sprinkle gelatin over water in cup, stand in small pan of simmering water, stir until gelatin is dissolved; cool slightly.

Combine gelatin mixture, sour cream, mayonnaise and cream in bowl, stir into pasta mixture; mix well. Press mixture into pan, cover, refrigerate overnight.

Serves 8.

■ Recipe can be made 2 days ahead.
■ Storage: Covered, in refrigerator.
■ Freeze: Not suitable.
■ Microwave: Suitable.

SWEET CHILI DUCK AND CARROT BAGELS

2 cups (about 6oz) chopped Chinese barbequed duck
2½ tablespoons dry sherry
1 tablespoon hoisin sauce
1½ tablespoons barbeque sauce
1½ tablespoons sweet chili sauce
1 carrot
1 green onion, sliced
6 bagels

Combine duck, sherry and sauces in bowl, cover, refrigerate 1 hour. Cut carrot into thin sticks, boil, steam or microwave until almost tender; drain. Rinse carrot under cold water; drain. Combine carrot and onion with duck mixture.

Cut each bagel in half. Divide duck mixture between bagel bases, cover with bagel tops. Place bagels onto greased baking sheet; cover with foil. Bake in 350°F oven about 20 minutes or until heated through.

Serves 6.

■ Recipe best made just before serving.
■ Freeze: Not suitable.
■ Microwave: Carrot suitable.

TARRAGON DUCK SALAD

2 boneless duck breast halves
all-purpose flour
1½ tablespoons vegetable oil
¼lb snow peas
1 apple chopped
3 green onions, chopped
1 hard-boiled egg, chopped
⅓ cup mayonnaise
⅓ cup sour cream
¼ cup heavy cream
1 tablespoon chopped fresh tarragon
½ teaspoon seeded mustard
4 Boston lettuce leaves

Toss duck in flour, shake away excess flour. Heat oil in pan, add duck, cook over high heat until well browned on both sides but still pink in the center, drain on absorbent paper; cool. Remove and discard skin and fat from duck, thinly slice duck meat.

Boil, steam or microwave snow peas until just tender, drain; slice.

Combine duck, snow peas, apple, onions and egg; mix well. Add combined mayonnaise, sour cream, cream, tarragon and mustard; mix well. Spoon salad into lettuce leaves.

Serves 4.

■ Recipe best made on day of serving.
■ Storage: Covered, in refrigerator.
■ Freeze: Not suitable.
■ Microwave: Peas suitable.

LEFT: Clockwise from left: Tarragon Duck Salad, Sweet Chili Duck and Carrot Bagels, Turkey Waldorf Ring.

top with strips of cucumber, onion and duck meat, roll pancakes to enclose filling.

Pancakes: Sift flour into bowl, stir in seeds, add combined boiling water and oil all at once, mix to a soft dough. Knead dough for 3 minutes on lightly floured surface until smooth. Cover, stand 15 minutes. Roll dough into a sausage shape, cut dough evenly into 12 portions, roll each portion into a 6 inch round. Heat heavy-based pan, dry-fry pancakes on both sides about 20 seconds or until lightly browned; keep warm.

Serves 4.

- Duck best cooked on day of serving. Pancakes can be made a day ahead.
- Storage: Duck, covered, in refrigerator. Unfilled pancakes, covered, in refrigerator.
- Freeze: Unfilled pancakes suitable.
- Microwave: Not suitable.

SIMMERED QUAIL WITH ORANGE AND HERB SAUCE

6 quail
½ teaspoon grated orange zest
1 cup fresh orange juice
½ cup water
**1 small chicken bouillon
    cube, crumbled**
½ cup dry white wine
¼ teaspoon dried marjoram leaves
**1½ tablespoons chopped
    fresh parsley**
½ cup heavy cream

Tie quail legs together with kitchen string. Combine zest, juice, water, bouillon cube, wine and herbs in pan. Bring to boil, add quail, simmer, covered, about 15 minutes or until quail are just tender. Remove quail, keep warm. Simmer liquid in pan, uncovered, until reduced to about ½ cup. Add cream, stir until heated through. Pour sauce over quail just before serving.

Serves 6.

- Recipe can be made 2 hours ahead.
- Storage: Covered, at room temperature.
- Freeze: Not suitable.
- Microwave: Not suitable.

SHREDDED DUCK WITH SESAME PANCAKES

3lb duck
¼ cup dark brown sugar
2½ tablespoons water
1½ tablespoons brown vinegar
**1 large green cucumber,
    peeled, seeded**
6 green onions
2½ tablespoons hoisin sauce
2 teaspoons honey

PANCAKES
1 cup all-purpose flour
1 tablespoon sesame seeds
½ cup boiling water
½ teaspoon Oriental sesame oil

Lower duck into large pan of boiling water, cover, bring to boil, remove duck from water. Pat duck dry with absorbent paper, stand at room temperature until cold.

Place duck on wire rack in roasting pan. Brush duck evenly with half the combined sugar, water and vinegar, refrigerate, uncovered, overnight.

Next day, brush duck with remaining sugar mixture, leave, uncovered, to dry. Bake in 350°F oven about 1½ hours, turning occasionally, or until duck is well browned and tender. Cut cucumber and onions into thin strips. Remove duck meat from bones, leaving skin on meat; shred finely. Discard bones.

Just before serving, spread warm pancakes with combined sauce and honey,

ABOVE: Shredded Duck with Sesame Pancakes.
RIGHT: Simmered Quail with Orange and Herb Sauce.

CHICKEN OMELETS WITH SWEET AND SOUR SAUCE

8 eggs, lightly beaten
1 cup (5oz) chopped cooked chicken
1 cup mung bean sprouts
4 green onions, chopped
2 teaspoons grated gingerroot
2 cloves garlic, minced
1 teaspoon light soy sauce

SWEET AND SOUR SAUCE
1½ tablespoons cornstarch
½ cup water
15oz can crushed pineapple
½ teaspoon Oriental sesame oil
¼ cup chopped Chinese mixed pickles

Combine eggs, chicken, sprouts, onions, gingerroot, garlic and sauce in bowl; mix well. Pour ⅓ cup of egg mixture into heated greased small omelet pan. Cook until lightly browned underneath, turn omelet, brown on other side; turn onto plate, keep warm. Repeat with remaining egg mixture. Serve warm omelets with hot sweet and sour sauce.

Sweet and Sour Sauce: Blend cornstarch and water in small pan. Add undrained pineapple, sesame oil and pickles. Stir over heat until sauce boils and thickens; simmer 1 minute.

Serves 4.

- Omelets and sauce best made just before serving.
- Freeze: Not suitable.
- Microwave: Sauce suitable.

SMOKED CHICKEN DE LUXE

2¾lb chicken
1 cup (6½oz) rice
½ cup dark brown sugar
½ cup Chinese tea leaves
2½ tablespoons Szechuan pepper
6 star anise

Boil, steam or microwave chicken until tender. Combine remaining ingredients in bowl. Completely line a wok or large pan

MUSHROOM CHICKEN TARTLETS

Both doughs should be cold throughout preparation. If dough becomes difficult to handle, cover and refrigerate for 30 minutes before the next process.

CHICKEN FILLING
1oz Chinese dried mushrooms
¾ cup milk
½ cup heavy cream
2 eggs, lightly beaten
¾ cup chopped cooked chicken
4 green onions, chopped
½ small red bell pepper,
finely chopped

WATER DOUGH
¾ cup all-purpose flour
⅓ cup water, approximately

FAT DOUGH
½ cup all-purpose flour
½ cup (¼ lb) lard
½ cup (1 stick) butter

Chicken Filling: Place mushrooms in bowl, cover with boiling water, stand 20 minutes. Drain mushrooms, discard stems, slice caps finely.

Combine milk, cream and eggs in bowl, add mushrooms, chicken, onions and pepper; mix well.

To make tarts, place water dough rectangle on 1 end of fat dough rectangle.

Fold other end of fat dough over to cover water dough.

Turn dough around so that the fold is on your left-hand side, roll to a 5 inch x 12 inch rectangle.

Fold narrow ends of dough in to meet in the center.

Fold in half again at the center. Repeat rolling and folding 3 more times, making sure that the fold is always on your left-hand side.

Roll dough to about ⅛ inch thickness, cut into 20 x 3½ inch rounds, ease rounds into greased deep, 3 inch fluted tartlet pans. Place pans on baking sheets, spoon in chicken filling then egg mixture. Bake in 400°F oven 10 minutes, reduce heat to 375°F; bake further 20 minutes or until egg mixture is set.

Water Dough: Sift flour into bowl, stir in enough water to mix to a firm dough. Knead dough on lightly floured surface until smooth. Roll to a 3½ inch x 5 inch rectangle. Wrap rectangle carefully in plastic wrap, refrigerate 30 minutes.

Fat Dough: Sift flour into bowl, rub in lard and butter, mix to a soft dough. Wrap in plastic wrap, refrigerate 30 minutes or until firm. Roll dough on floured surface to a 5 inch x 6 inch rectangle.

Makes about 20.

■ Tartlets can be made a day ahead.
■ Storage: Covered, in refrigerator.
■ Freeze: Not suitable.
■ Microwave: Not suitable.

with foil, place rice mixture in wok, place a rack over rice mixture. Place cooked chicken on rack, cover with tight-fitting lid. Smoke over high heat about 12 minutes, or until well browned all over. Discard rice mixture. Serve smoked chicken warm or cold.

Serves 4.

■ Chicken can be smoked 2 days ahead.
■ Storage: Covered, in refrigerator.
■ Freeze: Not suitable.
■ Microwave: Not suitable.

ABOVE: Clockwise from right: Chicken Omelets with Sweet and Sour Sauce, Smoked Chicken de Luxe, Mushroom Chicken Tartlets.

COLD ROCK CORNISH HENS WITH FIVE HERB DRESSING

4 x ¾lb Rock Cornish hens
2½ tablespoons butter
1 cup vegetable oil
4 green onions, chopped
1½ tablespoons chopped
    fresh chives
1½ tablespoons chopped
    fresh parsley
1 tablespoon chopped fresh tarragon
1½ tablespoons chopped fresh basil
1 tablespoon chopped fresh mint
⅓ cup white vinegar
2½ tablespoons tomato ketchup
1½ tablespoons Worcestershire
    sauce

Tie hens legs together, tuck wings under. Place hens on wire rack in roasting pan, brush with butter, bake in 350°F oven about 45 minutes or until cooked through. Transfer to shallow dish.

Combine remaining ingredients in jug, pour over hot hens. Spoon herb mixture over hens during cooling time. Refrigerate until cold. Serve cold hens with dressing.

Serves 8.

- Recipe can be made a day ahead.
- Storage: Covered, in refrigerator.
- Freeze: Not suitable.
- Microwave: Not suitable.

GLAZED TURKEY BUFFE WITH BACON MUFFINS

5lb frozen turkey buffe, thawed
1 tablespoon vegetable oil

FRUIT GLAZE
1 tablespoon butter
1 small onion, chopped
¼ cup chopped dried figs
¼ cup chopped dried apricots
⅔ cup fresh orange juice
2 teaspoons tomato paste
1 tablespoon dark brown sugar

BACON MUFFINS
6oz slices bacon, chopped
½ cup self-rising flour
1 teaspoon double-acting
    baking powder
2 cups (7oz) packaged unseasoned
    bread crumbs
1½ tablespoons chopped fresh sage
1¼ cups canned creamed corn
2 apples, peeled, grated
1 cup milk
2 eggs, separated

Place turkey buffe in greased roasting pan, brush with oil, cover with foil. Bake in 350°F oven 1¼ hours, remove foil, brush with fruit glaze and bake further 30 minutes or until cooked through. Stand 10 minutes before slicing. Serve turkey buffe with hot bacon muffins.

Fruit Glaze: Melt butter in pan, add onion, cook, stirring, until soft. Add remaining ingredients, bring to boil, simmer, uncovered, about 5 minutes or until thick and pulpy, stirring occasionally. Blend or process until smooth.

Bacon Muffins: Cook bacon in pan, stirring, until crisp; drain. Sift flour and baking powder into bowl, add bacon, bread crumbs, sage and corn. Squeeze excess moisture from apples using absorbent paper. Add apples, milk and egg yolks to bowl, stir until combined. Beat egg whites in small bowl until soft peaks form. Fold egg whites into corn mixture. Spoon mixture into well greased 6 x ¾ cup muffin tins. Bake in 350°F oven on low shelf under turkey about 35 minutes or until muffins are firm.

Serves 10.

- Turkey best cooked just before serving. Glaze can be made 2 days ahead.
- Storage: Glaze, covered, in refrigerator.
- Freeze: Muffins suitable.
- Microwave: Not suitable.

LEFT: From top: Glazed Turkey Buffe with Bacon Muffins, Cold Rock Cornish Hens with Five Herb Dressing.

CRISPY DUCK SALAD WITH CRUNCHY CROUTONS

4 boneless duck breast halves
1 tablespoon olive oil
1 clove garlic, minced
1½ tablespoons Italian
    salad dressing
1 radicchio lettuce
1 Boston lettuce
1 oak leaf lettuce
12 cherry tomatoes
⅓ cup grated fresh
    Parmesan cheese

CROUTONS
4 slices whole-wheat bread
1 tablespoon olive oil
¼ cup (½ stick) butter, melted
2 cloves garlic, minced

ANCHOVY DRESSING
2½oz can anchovy fillets, drained
1 clove garlic, minced
1 teaspoon French mustard
2½ tablespoons water
1½ tablespoons lemon juice
1 egg yolk
½ cup olive oil

Remove skin and fat from duck, discard fat; cut skin into thin strips. Place skin in pan, cook, stirring occasionally, until well browned and crisp. Remove duck skin from pan with slotted spoon; drain on absorbent paper.

Heat oil and garlic in pan, add duck fillets, cook until well browned all over and tender; drain. Slice duck thinly, combine with salad dressing in bowl; cool.

Just before serving, combine duck skin and meat with the lettuce leaves, tomatoes, cheese and croutons in bowl, toss well; top with anchovy dressing.
Croutons: Remove crusts from bread, cut bread into ½ inch cubes. Combine oil, butter and garlic in bowl, add bread, toss to coat evenly. Spread cubes on baking sheet, bake in 350°F oven about 15 minutes, tossing occasionally, or until croutons are lightly browned and crisp.
Anchovy Dressing: Blend anchovies, garlic, mustard, water, juice and egg yolk until well combined. Add oil in a thin stream while motor is operating, blend until thick.

Serves 6.

- Recipe can be prepared 6 hours ahead.
- Storage: Duck skin and meat, covered, in refrigerator. Croutons, in airtight container.
- Freeze: Not suitable.
- Microwave: Not suitable.

SMOKED TURKEY WITH CRANBERRY LIME MAYONNAISE

2lb smoked turkey breast roll

CRANBERRY LIME MAYONNAISE
1 cup mayonnaise
2 teaspoons cranberry sauce
1 tablespoon finely chopped
    dill pickle
1 tablespoon chopped fresh chives
1 teaspoon grated lime zest
2 teaspoons lime juice

Slice turkey, serve with cranberry lime mayonnaise.
Cranberry Lime Mayonnaise: Combine all ingredients in bowl; mix well.

Serves 6.

- Mayonnaise can be made a day ahead.
- Storage: Covered, in refrigerator.
- Freeze: Not suitable.

CHICKEN, CRANBERRY AND PISTACHIO PIES

1½ tablespoons butter
2½ tablespoons all-purpose flour
¾ cup water
2 small chicken bouillon
    cubes, crumbled
3 cups (15 oz) chopped
    cooked chicken
⅓ cup cranberry sauce
¼ cup chopped pistachios
2½ tablespoons chopped
    fresh chives
1 egg yolk, lightly beaten

PASTRY
2 cups all-purpose flour
5 oz (1¼ sticks) butter
1 egg, lightly beaten
½ cup water, approximately

Lightly oil 6 x ¾ cup muffin tins.

Melt butter in pan, add flour, stir until bubbling. Remove from heat, gradually stir in combined water and bouillon cubes. Stir over heat until sauce boils and thickens. Remove from heat, stir in chicken, sauce, nuts and chives; cool.

Roll two-thirds of the pastry on lightly floured surface to a 12 inch x 18 inch rectangle. Cut out 6 x 6 inch rounds from pastry. Ease rounds into prepared tins. Spoon chicken mixture into pastry cases.

Roll remaining pastry to an 8 inch x 12 inch rectangle, cut 6 x 4 inch rounds. Brush each round with egg yolk, place egg-side-down onto pies; press edges firmly to seal. Brush with remaining egg yolk, prick with skewer. Bake in 350°F oven about 40 minutes or until well browned and crisp. Stand pies 5 minutes before turning out.
Pastry: Sift flour into bowl, rub in butter. Add egg and enough water to make a soft dough. Turn dough onto floured surface, knead lightly until smooth. Cover dough, refrigerate 30 minutes.

Makes 6.

- Pies can be made a day ahead.
- Storage: Covered, in refrigerator.
- Freeze: Uncooked pies suitable.
- Microwave: Not suitable.

LEFT: Crispy Duck Salad with Crunchy Croutons.
RIGHT: From top: Chicken, Cranberry and Pistachio Pies, Smoked Turkey with Cranberry Lime Mayonnaise.

DUCK VOL-AU-VENTS WITH HERBED SOUR CREAM

3¾lb duck
4 x 5in vol-au-vent cases
1½ tablespoons olive oil
1 onion, chopped
2 cloves garlic, minced
2 oz cabanossi, chopped
14½oz can tomatoes
½ teaspoon sugar
2½ tablespoons chopped pitted
    black olives

HERBED SOUR CREAM
½ cup sour cream
1½ tablespoons chopped fresh basil
1½ tablespoons chopped
    fresh chives

Place duck on wire rack in roasting pan, bake in 350°F oven about 1½ hours or until tender; cool. Remove skin and fat from duck, remove meat from bones; discard skin, fat and bones. Slice duck meat.

Place vol-au-vent cases on baking sheet, bake in 350° oven about 5 minutes or until crisp. Heat oil in pan, add onion and garlic, cook, stirring, until onion is soft. Add cabanossi, cook further 1 minute. Stir in undrained crushed tomatoes, sugar and duck meat. Bring to boil, simmer, uncovered, about 5 minutes or until thickened; stir in olives.

Just before serving, spoon mixture into hot vol-au-vent cases, top with herbed sour cream.

Herbed Sour Cream: Combine all ingredients in bowl; mix well.

Serves 4.

- Duck mixture can be made a day ahead.
- Storage: Covered, in refrigerator.
- Freeze: Not suitable.
- Microwave: Not suitable.

PEPPERED QUAIL BREAST AND BACON SALAD

6 quail breasts
⅓ cup olive oil
2½ tablespoons dry red wine
2½ tablespoons ginger
    barbeque sauce
1 teaspoon white vinegar
1½ teaspoons seasoned pepper
1 teaspoon paprika
¼ teaspoon chili powder
6oz slices bacon, chopped
1 red leaf lettuce
1 Boston lettuce
12 cherry tomatoes, halved
2 green onions, chopped
⅓ cup grated fresh Parmesan cheese

BALSAMIC DRESSING
2½ tablespoons balsamic vinegar
1½ teaspoons seeded mustard
1½ tablespoons chopped
    fresh tarragon
½ cup olive oil

Combine quail breasts, half the oil, wine, sauce, vinegar, pepper, paprika and chili in bowl. Cover, refrigerate several hours or overnight.

Heat 1½ tablespoons of the remaining oil in pan, add bacon, cook, stirring, until crisp; drain on absorbent paper. Drain quail from marinade, discard marinade. Heat remaining oil in pan, add quail, cook until lightly browned all over and just tender; drain on absorbent paper.

Combine bacon and quail in bowl. Add torn lettuce, tomatoes and onions. Pour over balsamic dressing; toss well. Sprinkle with cheese.

Balsamic Dressing: Combine all ingredients in bowl; mix well.

Serves 4.

- Salad can be made 2 hours ahead.
- Storage: Covered, in refrigerator.
- Freeze: Not suitable.
- Microwave: Not suitable.

LEMON COCONUT ROCK CORNISH HENS

2 x ¾lb Rock Cornish hens
1 teaspoon curry powder
½ teaspoon ground cinnamon
1 teaspoon turmeric
2 teaspoons grated lemon zest
1 tablespoon coconut
2 teaspoons dark brown sugar
2½ tablespoons tomato paste
1½ tablespoons lemon juice
1⅔ cups canned unsweetened
    coconut milk

FIGGY RICE
2½ tablespoons vegetable oil
1 onion, finely chopped
1 clove garlic, minced
1 cup long-grain rice
1 cup (6oz) chopped dried figs
1 teaspoon turmeric
¼ teaspoon ground cloves
3¾ cups water
1 red bell pepper, chopped

Remove and discard wing tips of hens. Cut hens in half. Combine curry powder, cinnamon, turmeric, zest, coconut, sugar, paste, juice and milk in large bowl, add hens; mix well. Cover, refrigerate several hours or overnight.

Just before serving, remove hens from marinade, discard marinade. Broil hens until well browned and tender. Serve hens with figgy rice.

Figgy Rice: Heat oil in pan, add onion and garlic, cook, stirring, until onion is soft. Add rice, cook, stirring, 30 seconds. Add figs, turmeric, cloves and water, bring to boil, simmer, covered, about 12 minutes or until rice is tender and liquid is absorbed. Remove from heat, stir in pepper.

Serves 4.

- Hens can be prepared 2 days ahead. Rice can be made a day ahead.
- Storage: Covered, in refrigerator.
- Freeze: Marinated hens and prepared rice suitable.
- Microwave: Rice suitable.

LEFT: Clockwise from top: Peppered Quail Breast and Bacon Salad, Duck Vol-au-Vents with Herbed Sour Cream, Lemon Coconut Rock Cornish Hens.

BUTTERFLIED CHICKEN WITH HERB BUTTER

3lb chicken
3oz (¾ stick) butter
**2½ tablespoons chopped
    fresh parsley**
1 tablespoon chopped fresh dill
2 teaspoons chopped fresh thyme
1 teaspoon French mustard
¼lb slices bacon, chopped
1 clove garlic, minced
1½ tablespoons butter, melted, extra

TOMATO SAUCE
1½ tablespoons butter
1 onion, chopped
1 clove garlic, minced
14½oz can tomatoes
½ cup dry white wine
1½ tablespoons tomato paste

Using sharp knife or scissors, cut along backbone of chicken, turn chicken over, flatten with hand. Beat butter in small bowl until soft, beat in herbs, mustard, bacon and garlic.

Loosen skin of chicken by sliding hand between skin and meat at the neck joint. Spoon butter mixture under skin, work it evenly over legs and breast.

Just before serving, brush chicken with extra butter, place in roasting pan, bake in 350°F oven about 1¼ hours or until tender. Serve with tomato sauce.

Tomato Sauce: Heat butter in pan, add onion and garlic, cook, stirring, until onion is soft. Add undrained crushed tomatoes, wine and paste. Bring to boil, simmer, uncovered, about 5 minutes or until sauce is slightly thickened.

Serves 4.

- ■ Chicken can be prepared
  2 days ahead.
- ■ Storage: Covered, in refrigerator.
- ■ Freeze: Prepared chicken suitable.
- ■ Microwave: Not suitable.

OLIVE AND PIMIENTO CHICKEN IN PHYLLO

½ bunch (10oz) spinach
**1 (about 3oz) canned
    pimiento, drained**
1 small zucchini
4 chicken thighs, boned, skinned
6 pitted black olives, halved
4 slices mozzarella cheese
12 sheets phyllo pastry
3oz (¾ stick) butter, melted
1½ tablespoons sesame seeds

CREAMY MUSTARD SAUCE
¼ cup heavy cream
2½ tablespoons sour cream
¼ teaspoon dry mustard
1 teaspoon seeded mustard
2 teaspoons chopped fresh chives

Add spinach to pan of boiling water, drain immediately, rinse under cold water; drain spinach well.

Cut pimiento and zucchini into strips.

Place chicken fillets smooth-side-down on bench, pound gently between plastic wrap to flatten slightly. Divide pimiento, zucchini, olives and cheese crossways over center of fillets, fold fillets in half to enclose filling. Roll each fillet in 5 overlapped spinach leaves.

Layer 3 sheets of pastry, brushing each with butter. Place 1 prepared fillet at narrow end of pastry, roll once, fold in sides, continue rolling to form a parcel. Brush with more butter, sprinkle with seeds, place on greased baking sheet. Repeat with remaining pastry, butter, prepared fillets and seeds.

Just before serving, bake in 350°F oven about 10 minutes or until lightly browned, cover with foil, bake further 35 minutes or until pastry is well browned and chicken is cooked through. Serve chicken with creamy mustard sauce.

Creamy Mustard Sauce: Combine all ingredients in bowl; mix well.

Serves 4.

- ■ Recipe can be prepared a day ahead.
- ■ Storage: Covered, in refrigerator.
- ■ Freeze: Uncooked prepared
  fillets suitable.
- ■ Microwave: Not suitable.

LEFT: From left: Butterflied Chicken with Herb Butter, Olive and Pimiento Chicken in Phyllo. BELOW: Turkey Breast Roll with Fresh Tomato Relish.

TURKEY BREAST ROLL WITH FRESH TOMATO RELISH

2½ tablespoons vegetable oil
2lb turkey breast roll

FRESH TOMATO RELISH
2 tablespoons (¼ stick) butter
1 tablespoon black mustard seeds
1 onion, chopped
1lb ripe tomatoes, peeled
**½ cup canned drained
    chopped pimientos**
1 teaspoon sugar

Heat oil in roasting pan, add turkey, brown well all over. Bake in 350°F oven about 1 hour or until cooked through. Cover with foil, stand 10 minutes before slicing. Serve with fresh tomato relish.

Fresh Tomato Relish: Heat butter in pan, add seeds, cover, cook 1 minute. Add onion, cook, stirring, until onion is soft. Add finely chopped tomatoes, pimientos and sugar, cook, stirring, 5 minutes or until slightly thickened.

Serves 6.

- ■ Turkey best cooked just before
  serving. Relish can be made 2
  days ahead.
- ■ Storage: Covered, in refrigerator.
- ■ Freeze: Not suitable.
- ■ Microwave: Not suitable.

FAMILY LUNCHES

Quick, convenient and popular, these recipes all use readily available cuts, ground or cooked chicken so you can put them together with fuss-free ease. There are tasty drumsticks and wings, big burgers, croquettes and salads brimming with flavor. Schnitzels, too, are on the menu, as are golden brown pasties. For a change, consider novelties such as paper-wrapped chicken, and the easiest-ever deep-fried chicken rolls – just wrap in packaged pastry and cook. The food is mostly portable and could happily be taken for school or work lunches, as well!

CRUNCHY ONION CHICKEN WINGS

12 (about 2lb) chicken wings
all-purpose four
2 eggs, lightly beaten
1 cup (3½oz) packaged, unseasoned
    bread crumbs
2 teaspoons French onion dry soup mix
1 teaspoon grated lemon zest
2½ tablespoons vegetable oil

BARBEQUE SAUCE
¾ cup tomato ketchup
1 small onion, finely chopped
1½ tablespoons barbeque sauce
1½ tablespoons chutney

Gently cut wings at joints without cutting through wings, straighten wings. Toss wings in flour, shake away excess flour. Dip wings in eggs, then in combined bread crumbs, dry soup mix and zest.

Just before serving, place wings on baking sheet, brush with oil. Bake in 350°F oven about 30 minutes or until wings are browned and cooked through. Serve with barbeque sauce.

Barbeque Sauce: Combine all ingredients in bowl; mix well.

Serves 4.

■ Wings can be prepared a day ahead.
■ Storage: Covered, in refrigerator.
■ Freeze: Uncooked crumbed
  wings suitable.
■ Microwave: Not suitable.

RABBIT AND CHICKEN PASTIES

10oz rabbit pieces
1½ tablespoons olive oil
1 onion, finely chopped
½lb chicken thighs, boned, skinned,
    finely chopped
1 small potato, finely chopped
½ red bell pepper, finely chopped
1 bay leaf
1½ tablespoons tomato paste
1 cup dry red wine
1½ tablespoons chutney
1½ tablespoons chopped fresh basil
6 sheets ready-rolled puff pastry
1 egg yolk
1½ tablespoons milk

Remove rabbit meat from bones, discard bones, chop meat finely. Heat oil in pan, add rabbit meat, onion and chicken. Cook, stirring occasionally, about 10 minutes or until chicken is lightly browned. Add potato, pepper, bay leaf, paste and wine. Bring to boil, simmer, uncovered, about 25 minutes or until potato is soft and mixture is thickened. Stir in chutney and basil; cool. Discard bay leaf.

Cut pastry into 4½ inch rounds, top each round with a rounded tablespoon of chicken mixture. Lightly brush edges with combined egg yolk and milk, fold up edges, pinch together firmly to seal.

Place pasties on lightly greased baking sheets, brush with remaining egg yolk mixture. Bake in 350°F oven for about 35 minutes or until pasties are puffed and well browned.

Makes about 24.

■ Pasties can be prepared a
  day ahead.
■ Storage: Covered, in refrigerator.
■ Freeze: Uncooked pasties suitable.
■ Microwave: Not suitable.

RIGHT: From left: Rabbit and Chicken Pasties, Crunchy Onion Chicken Wings.

BRAISED CHICKEN WITH ANCHOVIES

2lb chicken pieces
all-purpose flour
2½ tablespoons olive oil
1 onion, sliced
1 clove garlic, minced
¾ cup dry white wine
¾ cup water
1 small chicken bouillon
    cube, crumbled
2 teaspoons dried oregano
1 bay leaf
6 pitted black olives, chopped
2 anchovy fillets, drained, chopped
2 canned red pimientos,
    drained, sliced
1½ tablespoons chopped
    fresh parsley

Toss chicken in flour, shake away excess flour. Heat oil in large pan, add chicken. Cook until well browned all over; remove from pan. Add onion and garlic to pan, cook, stirring, until onion is lightly browned. Add wine, water, bouillon cube, oregano and bay leaf. Bring to boil, add chicken, simmer, covered, about 30 minutes or until chicken is tender.

Just before serving, add olives, anchovies and pimientos to pan, stir until heated through. Discard bay leaf and stir in parsley.

Serves 4.

■ Recipe can be prepared a day ahead.
■ Storage: Covered, in refrigerator.
■ Freeze: Suitable.
■ Microwave: Suitable.

SATAY CHICKEN DRUMSTICKS

2 onions, chopped
2½ tablespoons vegetable oil
½ cup chunky peanut butter
2½ tablespoons sweet chili sauce
2½ tablespoons light soy sauce
¼ cup roasted unsalted peanuts
8 chicken drumsticks
⅓ cup sour cream

Blend or process onions, oil, peanut butter, sauces and peanuts until combined. Place drumsticks on baking sheet, brush with some of the satay mixture. Bake, uncovered, in 350°F oven 10 minutes. Turn chicken, brush with a little more satay mixture, bake, uncovered, further 25 minutes or until drumsticks are browned and cooked through.

Combine remaining satay mixture and sour cream in pan, bring to boil. Serve drumsticks with satay sauce.

Serves 4.

■ Recipe can be made a day ahead.
■ Storage: Covered, in refrigerator.
■ Freeze: Not suitable.
■ Microwave: Suitable.

PAPER-WRAPPED CHICKEN

8 chicken thighs, boned, skinned
2½ tablespoons light soy sauce
2 teaspoons sugar
2½ tablespoons dry sherry
¼ teaspoon five-spice powder
2 teaspoons Oriental sesame oil
1 teaspoons grated gingerroot
8 Chinese dried mushrooms
2 dried Chinese pork sausages
⅓ cup canned sliced bamboo
    shoots, drained
4 green onions, halved

Combine chicken fillets with sauce, sugar, sherry, spice powder, oil and gingerroot in large bowl, cover; refrigerate several hours or overnight. Place mushrooms in bowl, cover with boiling water, stand 20 minutes. Drain mushrooms, discard stems, chop caps finely. Chop each sausage into 4 pieces. Cut 4 x 10½ inch rounds of baking paper.

Drain fillets, discard marinade. Place 1 fillet onto each paper round, top with some of the mushrooms, some of the bamboo shoots and another fillet, then with 2 pieces sausage and 2 pieces onion.

Fold paper over fillets, roll and fold paper around edge, tuck end underneath. Repeat with remaining fillets, mushrooms, bamboo shoots, onions and sausages.

Place parcels onto baking sheet, bake in 350°F oven about 25 minutes or until fillets are tender.

Serves 4.

■ Recipe can be prepared a day ahead.
■ Storage: Covered, in refrigerator.
■ Freeze: Not suitable.
■ Microwave: Suitable.

LEFT: Clockwise from right: Paper-Wrapped Chicken, Braised Chicken with Anchovies, Satay Chicken Drumsticks.

CRISPY NOODLE SALAD WITH BARBEQUED CHICKEN

2 x 3oz packaged chicken-flavored
2 minute noodles
oil for deep-frying
¼ teaspoon five-spice powder
2 barbequed chicken breast quarters
1 red bell pepper, chopped
2 green onions, chopped
½ cup bean sprouts

DRESSING
2 teaspoons grated gingerroot
1 teaspoon light soy sauce
1 teaspoon sugar
¼ teaspoon Oriental sesame oil

Add noodles to pan of boiling water, boil, uncovered, until noodles separate, drain well, rinse under cold water; drain on absorbent paper.

Deep-fry noodles in hot oil in batches until crisp and lightly browned; drain on absorbent paper. While still hot, sprinkle with combined flavor sachet (from noodles) and spice powder.

Remove skin from chicken, remove meat from bones, discard skin and bones; cut chicken meat into strips. Combine noodles, chicken, pepper, onions and sprouts in bowl; mix well.

Just before serving, sprinkle noodle salad with dressing.

Dressing: Press gingerroot between 2 teaspoons to extract juice; discard pulp. Combine juice, sauce, sugar and oil in jar; shake well.

Serves 4.

■ Best made close to serving.
■ Freeze: Not suitable.
■ Microwave: Not suitable.

SESAME CHICKEN TOASTIES

½lb ground chicken
1 clove garlic, minced
½ teaspoon ground gingerroot
2 teaspoons cornstarch
1 egg white, lightly beaten
6 thin slices white bread
¼ cup sesame seeds
oil for deep-frying

Combine chicken, garlic, gingerroot, cornstarch and egg white in bowl. Remove crusts from bread; spread chicken mixture over 1 side of each slice. Dip bread, chicken-side-down into sesame seeds to coat.

Just before serving, deep-fry chicken toasties in hot oil until well browned; drain on absorbent paper.

Makes 24.

■ Toasties can be prepared 3 hours ahead.
■ Storage: Covered, in refrigerator.
■ Freeze: Uncooked toasties suitable.
■ Microwave: Not suitable.

CHICKEN, CHEESE AND CORN BURGERS

4oz cheddar cheese
1lb ground chicken
2 green onions, chopped
1 cup (3½oz) packaged, unseasoned
bread crumbs
1 egg, lightly beaten
4½oz can whole-kernel corn, drained
all-purpose flour
1 egg, lightly beaten, extra
1½ tablespoons milk
¾ cup packaged, unseasoned
bread crumbs, extra
2 small chicken bouillon
cubes, crumbled
2½ tablespoons vegetable oil
6 hamburger buns
6 lettuce leaves
6 slices beet
1 avocado, sliced
1 tomato, sliced
2 radishes, sliced
¼ cup mayonnaise

Cut cheese into ¼ inch cubes. Combine cheese, chicken, onions, bread crumbs, egg and corn in bowl. Divide mixture into 6 portions, shape into patties. Toss patties lightly in flour, shake away excess flour. Dip in combined extra egg and milk, then into combined extra bread crumbs and bouillon cubes. Place patties on plate, cover, refrigerate 1 hour.

Heat oil in pan, add patties, cook until lightly browned and cooked through.

Just before serving, split and toast buns. Assemble burgers, using buns, patties, lettuce, beet, avocado, tomato, radishes and mayonnaise.

Makes 6.

■ Patties can be made a day ahead.
■ Storage: Covered, in refrigerator.
■ Freeze: Uncooked patties suitable.
■ Microwave: Not suitable.

RIGHT: Clockwise from left: Chicken, Cheese and Corn Burgers, Sesame Chicken Toasties, Crispy Noodle Salad with Barbequed Chicken.

CHICKEN, PASTA AND CASHEW SALAD

1½ tablespoons vegetable oil
4 boneless, skinless chicken
**   breast halves**
1 bunch (about ½lb) fresh
**   asparagus, chopped**
5oz rigatoni pasta
½ cup unsalted, roasted cashews
7½oz can pineapple
**   chunks, drained**
3 green onions, chopped
1 red bell pepper, chopped

DRESSING
2½ tablespoons light soy sauce
1 teaspoon dark brown sugar
¼ teaspoon Oriental sesame oil
½ teaspoon grated gingerroot

Heat oil in pan, add chicken fillets in single layer, cook until well browned all over and tender, drain; cool. Chop fillets coarsely.

Boil, steam or microwave asparagus until just tender, drain; cool. Add pasta to large pan of boiling water, boil, uncovered, until just tender, drain, rinse under cold water; drain.

Just before serving, combine chicken, asparagus, pasta, cashews, pineapple, onions and pepper in large bowl, pour over dressing; toss well.

Dressing: Combine all ingredients in jar; shake well.

Serves 4.

■ Salad and dressing can be made separately 6 hours ahead.
■ Storage: Covered, in refrigerator.
■ Freeze: Not suitable.
■ Microwave: Asparagus and pasta suitable.

TROPICAL CHICKEN SCHNITZELS

4 boneless, skinless chicken
**   breast halves**
all-purpose flour
1 egg, lightly beaten
2½ tablespoons milk
¾ cup packaged, unseasoned
**   bread crumbs**
oil for shallow-frying
1 cup (¼lb) grated cheddar cheese

SAUCE
1½ tablespoons vegetable oil
1 onion, chopped
2 tomatoes, peeled, finely chopped
2½oz cooked ham, chopped
½ cup canned, drained
**   crushed pineapple**
1½ tablespoons tomato paste

Flatten chicken slightly with meat mallet. Toss chicken in flour, shake away excess flour. Dip in combined egg and milk, then in bread crumbs to coat.

Heat oil in large pan, add chicken, cook until well browned all over and tender. Remove chicken from pan, place in single layer in shallow ovenproof dish. Spoon sauce over chicken, sprinkle with cheese, broil until cheese is melted.

Sauce: Heat oil in pan, add onion, cook, stirring, until soft. Add tomatoes, ham, pineapple and paste. Bring to boil, simmer, uncovered, about 5 minutes or until slightly thickened.

Serves 4.

■ Recipe can be made a day ahead.
■ Storage: Covered, in refrigerator.
■ Freeze: Uncooked crumbed fillets suitable.
■ Microwave: Not suitable.

GOLDEN DRUMSTICKS WITH HERB MAYONNAISE

12 chicken drumsticks
all-purpose flour
2 eggs, lightly beaten
1½ tablespoons milk
¾ cup packaged, unseasoned
**   bread crumbs**
oil for deep-frying

HERB MAYONNAISE
⅔ cup mayonnaise
⅓ cup thickened cream
2 teaspoons chopped fresh parsley
2 teaspoons chopped fresh chives
2 teaspoons chopped fresh tarragon

Toss chicken in flour, shake away excess flour. Dip in combined eggs and milk, then in bread crumbs.

Just before serving, deep-fry chicken in hot oil until well browned and cooked through; drain on absorbent paper. Serve with herb mayonnaise.

Herb Mayonnaise: Combine mayonnaise, cream and herbs in bowl; mix well.

Serves 4 to 6.

■ Chicken can be prepared a day ahead.
■ Storage: Covered, in refrigerator.
■ Freeze: Uncooked crumbed chicken suitable.
■ Microwave: Not suitable.

LEFT: Clockwise from top: Tropical Chicken Schnitzel, Golden Drumsticks with Herb Mayonnaise, Chicken, Pasta and Cashew Salad.

Place mushrooms in bowl, cover with boiling water, stand 20 minutes. Drain mushrooms, discard stems, chop caps finely. Combine mushrooms, chicken, egg, cornstarch and soy sauce in bowl, cover; stand 10 minutes.

Heat oil in wok or large pan, add chicken mixture and gingerroot, stir-fry about 5 minutes or until mixture is separated and cooked through. Add sesame oil, chestnuts, hoisin sauce, sherry and onions; stir-fry until heated through. Serve in lettuce leaves.

Serves 4.

- Chicken mixture can be made a day ahead.
- Storage: Covered, in refrigerator.
- Freeze: Chicken mixture suitable.
- Microwave: Not suitable.

CURRIED CHICKEN PASTIES

1 potato, chopped
1 carrot, chopped
3 boneless, skinless chicken breast
　　halves, finely chopped
1 onion, finely chopped
½ cup frozen peas
1 cup water
1 small chicken bouillon
　　cube, crumbled
1 tablespoon butter
1 tablespoon all-purpose flour
1 teaspoon curry powder
¼ teaspoon ground coriander
4 sheets ready-rolled puff pastry
1 tablespoon milk
1 egg yolk

Combine potato, carrot, chicken, onion, peas, water and bouillon cube in pan. Bring to boil, simmer, uncovered, about 15 minutes or until vegetables are soft, stirring occasionally. Remove from heat, drain; reserve ½ cup liquid.

Melt butter in pan, add flour, curry powder and coriander, cook, stirring, 1 minute. Remove from heat, gradually stir in reserved liquid. Stir over heat until mixture boils and thickens. Stir into chicken mixture; cool.

Cut a 6½ inch round from each sheet of pastry. Divide chicken mixture between rounds. Fold edges of pastry into center, pinch edges together to seal.

Place pasties on lightly greased baking sheet, brush with combined milk and egg yolk. Bake in 375°F oven about 20 minutes or until golden brown.

Serves 4.

- Filling can be made a day ahead.
- Storage: Covered, in refrigerator.
- Freeze: Uncooked pasties suitable.
- Microwave: Not suitable.

PASTA, RADICCHIO AND CHICKEN SALAD

1½ cups (4oz) pasta twists
2 cups (10oz) chopped,
　　cooked chicken
½ red bell pepper, finely chopped
¼lb mushrooms, thinly sliced
1 carrot, grated
1½ tablespoons chopped
　　flat-leafed parsley
1½ tablespoons chopped fresh basil
2 small radicchio lettuce
¼ cup grated fresh Parmesan cheese

CHILI LIME DRESSING
1 tablespoon sambal oelek
2 cloves garlic, minced
2½ tablespoons lime juice
¼ cup olive oil

Add pasta to large pan of boiling water, boil, uncovered, until just tender; drain, cool. Combine pasta, chicken, pepper, mushrooms, carrot, parsley and basil in bowl. Arrange leaves from 1 lettuce on serving plate. Tear remaining lettuce into bite-sized pieces, toss into salad. Add half the chili lime dressing to salad; mix well. Pile salad onto lettuce, drizzle with remaining dressing, sprinkle with cheese.
Chili Lime Dressing: Whisk ingredients together in bowl.

Serves 6.

- Recipe best made just before serving.
- Freeze: Not suitable.
- Microwave: Pasta suitable.

CHICKEN IN LETTUCE CUPS

8 Chinese dried mushrooms
1lb ground chicken
1 egg, lightly beaten
2 teaspoons cornstarch
1½ tablespoons light soy sauce
2½ tablespoons vegetable oil
1 teaspoon grated gingerroot
½ teaspoon Oriental sesame oil
¾ cup canned sliced water
　　chestnuts, drained, chopped
1½ tablespoons hoisin sauce
1 tablespoon dry sherry
2 green onions, chopped
4 lettuce leaves

*ABOVE: Pasta, Radicchio and Chicken Salad.
RIGHT: From top: Curried Chicken Pasties,
Chicken in Lettuce Cups.*

SPICY YOGURT CHICKEN

2lb chicken pieces
2 cups plain yogurt
3 cloves garlic, minced
2 teaspoons curry powder
2 teaspoons turmeric
2 teaspoons paprika
2 teaspoons garam marsala
¼ teaspoon chili powder
1 teaspoon ground cumin
1 teaspoon fennel seeds
2 teaspoons castor sugar

Place chicken in large bowl, mix in remaining ingredients; cover, refrigerate several hours or overnight.
Just before serving, broil chicken until browned all over and tender. Serve with extra yogurt, if desired.

Serves 4.

■ Chicken can be prepared
   2 days ahead.
■ Storage: Covered, in refrigerator.
■ Freeze: Marinated chicken suitable.
■ Microwave: Not suitable.

CHEESY CHICKEN POTATOES

4 large (7oz each) potatoes
1 tablespoon vegetable oil
1 cup (5oz) chopped cooked chicken
¼ red bell pepper, chopped
¼ green bell pepper, chopped
1 small chicken bouillon
   cube, crumbled
⅓ cup mayonnaise
2½ tablespoons butter, melted
1½ tablespoons chopped
   fresh chives
½ cup grated cheddar cheese
¼ teaspoon paprika

Scrub and dry potatoes, prick all over with fork. Place potatoes on baking sheet, bake in 350˚F oven about 1 hour or until soft. Cut potatoes in half crossways, scoop out pulp, leaving ¼ inch shell. Place potatoes on baking sheet, brush inside and out with oil, bake in 400˚F oven for 10 minutes.

Mash potato pulp in bowl, add chicken, peppers, bouillon cube, mayonnaise, butter and chives. Spoon mixture into potato shells, sprinkle with cheese and paprika. Bake in 350˚F oven about 15 minutes or until lightly browned.

Serves 4.

■ Recipe can be made a day ahead.
■ Storage: Covered, in refrigerator.
■ Freeze: Not suitable.
■ Microwave: Suitable.

CHICKEN, HAM AND CHEESE ROLLS

¾lb boneless, skinless chicken
   breast halves
1lb piece square, cooked ham
1lb processed cheddar cheese
1½ tablespoons all-purpose flour
2 tablespoons water
8oz packet egg roll skins
oil for deep-frying

Cut chicken into ½ inch strips. Cut ham and cheese into ½ inch strips the same length as chicken. Blend flour and water in bowl.

Place a strip of chicken, a strip of ham and a strip of cheese diagonally across 1 end of each skin, fold sides in, roll up firmly, brush tips of skins with flour paste; press lightly to seal. Deep-fry rolls in hot oil until lightly browned and cooked through; drain on absorbent paper.

Makes about 20.

■ Recipe can be prepared
   2 hours ahead.
■ Storage: Covered, in refrigerator.
■ Freeze: Uncooked rolls suitable.
■ Microwave: Not suitable.

RIGHT: Clockwise from right: Spicy Yogurt Chicken, Cheesy Chicken Potatoes, Chicken, Ham and Cheese Rolls.

BARBEQUES

The great thing about our barbeque recipes is that you can cook them in a conventional oven or broiler, as well. But there's nothing like the barbeque for unique smoky flavor, extra-crispy skins and lovely little brown bits to savor! We've done popular pick-up-and-eat-kabobs, drumsticks and wings slathered with flavor, plus heaps of other wonderfully tasty recipes. For example, stylish chicken and Rock Cornish hens, duck patties with salad, quenelle-filled chicken breasts with brandy sauce and lots of quail (one as easy as brushing quail with butter and hazelnuts). Then, for a bread winner, try chicken and cheese muffins!

SWEET AND SPICY CHICKEN KABOBS

1¼lb chicken thighs, boned, skinned
¼ cup light soy sauce
1½ tablespoons tomato ketchup
1 teaspoon chili sauce
2½ tablespoons honey
1 tablespoon dry sherry
1 teaspoon grated gingerroot
1 clove garlic, minced
1 red bell pepper, chopped
15oz can pineapple chunks, drained

Cut chicken into long, thin strips. Combine sauces, honey, sherry, gingerroot and garlic in bowl, add chicken; mix well. Cover, refrigerate mixture several hours or overnight.

Drain chicken; reserve marinade. Thread chicken, pepper and pineapple onto skewers. Barbeque or broil kabobs until chicken is tender, brushing kabobs occasionally with reserved marinade.

Makes about 12.
■ Recipe can be prepared a day ahead.
■ Storage: Covered, in refrigerator.
■ Freeze: Uncooked marinated chicken suitable.
■ Microwave: Not suitable.

TANDOORI-STYLE CHICKEN

1 teaspoon turmeric
½ teaspoon paprika
½ teaspoon garam masala
¼ teaspoon ground cardamom
¼ teaspoon chili powder
pinch saffron powder
1 clove garlic, minced
2 tablespoons brown vinegar
2 teaspoons dark brown sugar
¼ cup plain yogurt
6 boneless, skinless chicken breast halves

Combine spices, garlic, vinegar, sugar and yogurt in bowl, add chicken; mix well. Cover, refrigerate 3 hours or overnight.
Just before serving, cook chicken on heated, oiled barbeque plate or in pan until well browned and tender.

Serves 6.
■ Recipe can be prepared a day ahead.
■ Storage: Covered, in refrigerator.
■ Freeze: Uncooked marinated chicken suitable.
■ Microwave: Not suitable.

HOT AND SPICY CHICKEN DRUMSTICKS

1 cup tomato puree
1 clove garlic, minced
1 teaspoon sambal oelek
2 teaspoons paprika
2½ tablespoons olive oil
1 teaspoon ground cumin
2½ tablespoons sour cream
8 chicken drumsticks

Combine puree, garlic, sambal oelek, paprika, oil, cumin and sour cream in bowl; mix well. Brush drumsticks all over with tomato mixture. Cook drumsticks in covered barbeque or in 350°F oven about 30 minutes or until tender. Drumsticks can also be broiled; turn drumsticks frequently during cooking.

Serves 4.
■ Best made just before serving.
■ Freeze: Not suitable.
■ Microwave: Not suitable.

RIGHT: From top: Sweet and Spicy Chicken Kebabs, Hot and Spicy Chicken Drumsticks, Tandoori-Style Chicken.

DUCK PATTY SALAD WITH ORANGE VINAIGRETTE

1 Boston lettuce
3 oranges, segmented
⅔ cup pecans

PATTIES

1½lb boneless duck breast halves
1lb ground chicken
1 egg
½ cup packaged, unseasoned
     bread crumbs
2 teaspoons seeded mustard
2½ tablespoons chopped fresh chives
1 teaspoon chopped fresh thyme
1 small chicken bouillon
     cube, crumbled
1 cup (3½oz) packaged, unseasoned
     bread crumbs, extra
2 teaspoons chicken seasoning

ORANGE VINAIGRETTE

⅓ cup fresh orange juice
¼ cup olive oil
1 teaspoon grated orange zest
½ teaspoon French mustard
1½ tablespoons chopped fresh chives

Arrange lettuce, orange segments and nuts in serving dishes. Drizzle over dressing, arrange warm patties in salad, top with crispy duck skin.

Patties: Remove skin and fat in 1 piece from each duck fillet; reserve half the skin and fat. Chop duck meat, blend or process with chicken, egg, bread crumbs, mustard, herbs and bouillon cube until well combined. Roll rounded tablespoons of mixture into balls, toss in combined extra bread crumbs; flatten slightly. Place patties on tray, cover, refrigerate 30 minutes.

Cut reserved duck skin pieces into thin strips. Cook on oiled barbeque plate or in pan until well browned and crisp; drain on absorbent paper.

Cook patties on barbeque plate or in pan about 2 minutes each side or until well browned and cooked through. Place patties in bowl, toss with chicken seasoning.

Orange Vinaigrette: Combine all ingredients in jar; shake well.

Serves 6.

■ Patties can be made a day ahead.
     Skin best cooked just before serving.
■ Storage: Covered, in refrigerator.
■ Freeze: Uncooked and cooked
     patties suitable.
■ Microwave: Not suitable.

CHILI AND LEMON GRASS ROCK CORNISH HENS

2½ tablespoons sambal oelek
1½ tablespoons chopped fresh
     lemon grass
¾ cup canned, unsweetened
     coconut milk
1½ tablespoons chopped
     fresh cilantro
2 teaspoons grated gingerroot
2 cloves garlic, minced
½ teaspoon turmeric
4 x 1lb Rock Cornish hens, halved

Blend or process sambal oelek, lemon grass, coconut milk, cilantro, gingerroot, garlic and turmeric until almost smooth. Pour mixture over hens in dish, cover, refrigerate several hours or overnight, turning occasionally.

Drain hens, reserve marinade. Cook

hens on barbeque or broil until browned and tender. Brush with reserved marinade during cooking.

Serves 8.

◼ Recipe can be prepared 2 days ahead.
◼ Storage: Covered, in refrigerator.
◼ Freeze: Uncooked marinated hens suitable.
◼ Microwave: Not suitable.

LEFT: Duck Patty Salad with Orange Vinaigrette.
ABOVE: From left: Chili and Lemon Grass Rock Cornish Hens, Ginger Chicken Kebabs.

GINGER CHICKEN KABOBS

1¾lb chicken thighs, boned, skinned
1½ tablespoons grated gingerroot
⅓ cup light soy sauce
¼ cup lemon juice
2½ tablespoons vegetable oil
2½ tablespoons dark brown sugar
2 cloves garlic, minced
2½ tablespoons green ginger wine
3 zucchini, sliced
6oz (about 16) button mushrooms
2 teaspoons cornstarch
2 teaspoons water
½lb cherry tomatoes

Cut chicken into long ½inch strips. Press gingerroot between 2 spoons to extract juice; discard pulp. Combine gingerroot juice, sauce, lemon juice, oil, sugar, garlic and wine in bowl, add chicken. Cover, refrigerate several hours or overnight.

Drain chicken; reserve marinade. Thread chicken, zucchini and mushrooms onto skewers. Combine blended cornstarch and water with reserved marinade in pan, stir over heat until mixture boils and thickens. Barbeque or broil kabobs until tender, brushing frequently with marinade.
Just before serving, place cherry tomatoes on skewers.

Serves 6.

◼ Recipe can be prepared a day ahead.
◼ Storage: Covered, in refrigerator.
◼ Freeze: Uncooked marinated chicken suitable.
◼ Microwave: Not suitable.

MUSTARD ROSEMARY CHICKEN

¼ **cup lemon juice**
¾ **cup olive oil**
4 **cloves garlic, minced**
2½ **tablespoons French mustard**
1 **tablespoon dried rosemary leaves**
½ **teaspoon cracked black
   peppercorns**
12 **chicken thigh cutlets**

Combine juice, oil, garlic, mustard, rosemary and peppercorns in bowl. Add chicken, mix well, cover, refrigerate several hours or overnight.

Drain chicken, cook on barbeque or broil until well browned and tender.

Serves 6.

■ Recipe can be prepared
  2 days ahead.
■ Storage: Covered, in refrigerator.
■ Freeze: Uncooked marinated
  chicken suitable.
■ Microwave: Not suitable.

MINTED CHUTNEY ROCK CORNISH HENS

2½ **tablespoons olive oil**
¼ **cup lemon juice**
2½ **tablespoons chutney, strained**
1½ **tablespoons chopped fresh mint**
1 **teaspoon light soy sauce**
4 x 1lb **Rock Cornish hens, halved**

Combine oil, juice, chutney, mint, sauce and hens in bowl. Cover, refrigerate several hours or overnight, turning occasionally.

Remove hens from marinade; reserve marinade. Cook hens on barbeque or broil until well browned and tender. Brush with reserved marinade during cooking.

Serves 8.

■ Recipe can be prepared a day ahead.
■ Storage: Covered, in refrigerator.
■ Freeze: Uncooked marinated
  hens suitable.
■ Microwave: Not suitable.

HAZELNUT BUTTERED QUAIL

8 **quail**
1½ **tablespoons butter, melted**

HAZELNUT BUTTER
¼ **cup (½ stick) butter**
¼ **cup packaged ground hazelnuts**

Using sharp knife or scissors, cut down either side of backbone of quail; discard backbones. Brush quail with butter, cook on barbeque or broil until lightly browned and cooked through. Serve with sliced hazelnut butter.

Hazelnut Butter: Beat butter and hazelnuts in small bowl, spoon onto foil, roll up firmly, shape into sausage. Refrigerate until firm.

Serves 8.

■ Butter can be made 2 days ahead.
■ Storage: Covered, in refrigerator.
■ Freeze: Butter suitable.
■ Microwave: Not suitable.

LEFT: From left: Minted Chutney Rock Cornish Hen, Mustard Rosemary Chicken. ABOVE: Hazelnut Buttered Quail.

BARBEQUED CHICKEN WITH PEPPER HERB MARINADE

2½lb chicken, quartered

PEPPER HERB MARINADE
1 cup olive oil
½ cup dry white wine
2 teaspoons cracked black peppercorns
¼ cup fresh lemon juice
3 cloves garlic, minced
6 green onions, chopped
2 teaspoons chopped fresh rosemary
⅓ cup chopped fresh basil

Add chicken to marinade in bowl, mix well, cover, refrigerate overnight. Drain chicken; reserve marinade. Cook chicken in covered barbeque or in 350°F oven about 25 minutes or until browned and tender. Heat reserved marinade in pan, bring to boil, drizzle over chicken; serve with remaining marinade.

Pepper Herb Marinade: Combine all ingredients in shallow dish; mix well.

Serves 4.
- Can be prepared 2 days ahead.
- Storage: Covered, in refrigerator.
- Freeze: Uncooked marinated chicken suitable.
- Microwave: Not suitable.

MUSHROOM AND PORT QUAIL

6 quail
2 tablespoons (¼ stick) butter, melted

SEASONING
1 chicken thigh, boned, skinned
3½oz cooked ham, chopped
½ cup fresh bread crumbs
2½ tablespoons heavy cream
2 teaspoons chopped fresh basil

MUSHROOM AND PORT SAUCE
1 cup port wine
1 cup water
2 small chicken bouillon cubes, crumbled
2 green onions, chopped
½ teaspoon black peppercorns
2½ tablespoons butter
½lb mushrooms, thinly sliced
2 teaspoons chopped fresh basil
2 teaspoons cornstarch
1 tablespoon water, extra

Fill quail with seasoning, tie legs together; brush with butter. Cook quail in covered barbeque or in 350°F oven about 40 minutes or until lightly browned and cooked through. Serve with mushroom and port sauce.
Seasoning: Blend or process chicken, ham, bread crumbs and cream until smooth, stir in basil.

DEVILLED CHICKEN DRUMSTICKS

2½ tablespoons barbeque sauce
1 teaspoon dry mustard
1 teaspoon curry powder
2 tablespoons (¼ stick) butter, melted
8 chicken drumsticks

Combine sauce, mustard, curry powder and butter in bowl. Brush drumsticks all over with mustard mixture. Cook drumsticks in covered barbeque or 350°F oven about 30 minutes or until tender.

Serves 4.

■ Recipe best made just before serving.
■ Freeze: Not suitable.
■ Microwave: Not suitable.

CHICKEN PATTIES WITH MUSTARD CREAM

1lb ground chicken
¾ cup fresh bread crumbs
¼ cup chopped fresh parsley
2 teaspoons fresh thyme leaves
few drops Tabasco sauce
1 egg, lightly beaten
4 thick slices bacon

MUSTARD CREAM
⅔ cup sour cream
1 tablespoon seeded mustard
**2½ tablespoons chopped
    fresh chives**

Combine chicken, bread crumbs, herbs, sauce and egg in bowl; mix well. Shape mixture into 4 patties. Trim bacon, wrap around patties, secure with toothpicks or skewers. Place patties on tray, cover, refrigerate 1 hour.

Cook patties on oiled barbeque plate or in pan until cooked through. Serve with mustard cream.

Mustard Cream: Combine all ingredients in bowl; mix well.

Serves 4.

■ Patties can be prepared a day ahead.
■ Storage: Covered, in refrigerator.
■ Freeze: Uncooked patties suitable.
■ Microwave: Not suitable.

LEFT: Clockwise from right: Mushroom and Port Quail, Devilled Chicken Drumsticks, Barbequed Chicken with Pepper Herb Marinade.
BELOW: Chicken Patties with Mustard Cream.

Mushroom and Port Sauce: Combine port, water, bouillon cubes, onions and peppercorns in pan, bring to boil, simmer, uncovered, about 5 minutes or until reduced by half; strain. Heat butter in pan add mushrooms, cook, stirring, until mushrooms are well browned. Add port mixture, stir in basil then blended cornstarch and extra water. Stir over heat until sauce boils and thickens.

Serves 6.

■ Recipe can be prepared a day ahead.
■ Storage: Covered, in refrigerator.
■ Freeze: Uncooked seasoned quail suitable.
■ Microwave: Sauce suitable.

GARLIC APRICOT CHICKEN WINGS

12 (about 2lb) chicken wings
3 cloves garlic, minced
⅓ cup apricot jam, warmed

Tuck wing tips under wings to form triangles. Barbeque or broil wings until almost cooked. Brush with combined garlic and jam, continue cooking until tender.

Serves 4.

■ Recipe best made just before serving.
■ Freeze: Not suitable.
■ Microwave: Not suitable.

CARROT AND PECAN TURKEY ROLL

4lb boneless turkey breast half
2 carrots, coarsely grated
⅓ cup chopped glace pineapple
½ cup chopped pecans
½ cup fresh bread crumbs
1½ tablespoons chopped fresh mint
1 egg, lightly beaten
8 thick slices bacon

Carefully remove skin from turkey, reserve skin.

Cut horizontally through center of turkey without cutting completely in half.

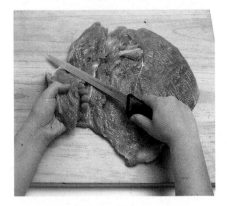

Cut thick portion of turkey horizontally without cutting completely through.

Lay this cut portion to overlap edge of main piece.

Cover turkey with plastic wrap, pound lightly with meat mallet to flatten. Spread turkey with combined carrots, pineapple, nuts, bread crumbs, mint and egg, leaving a ¾ inch border around edges. Roll turkey tightly, wrap roll in reserved skin, then in bacon. Wrap roll in foil, place on wire rack in roasting pan. Cook in covered barbeque or in 350°F oven 45 minutes, carefully remove foil from roll. Cook further 45 minutes or until tender. Cover roll with foil, stand 10 minutes before slicing. Serve sliced roll hot or cold.

Serves 8.

■ Roll can be made 2 days ahead.
■ Storage: Covered, in refrigerator.
■ Freeze: Uncooked roll suitable.
■ Microwave: Not suitable.

FRUITY QUAIL WITH BACON

8 quail
1½ tablespoons olive oil
1 onion, finely chopped
½ cup cooked rice
⅓ cup chopped dried apricots
⅓ cup chopped pitted prunes
2½ tablespoons chopped fresh parsley
4 thick slices bacon, halved
1½ tablespoons olive oil, extra

TOMATO SAUCE
1 tablespoon olive oil
1 onion, chopped
2 cloves garlic, minced
1 small fresh red chili pepper, chopped
14½oz can tomatoes
2½ tablespoons tomato paste
1 teaspoon sugar
¼ cup water

Bone quail following instructions in "Pre-Cooking Preparations" at the back of this book; leave legs and wings intact. Heat oil in pan, add onion, cook, stirring, until soft. Combine onion mixture, rice, apricots, prunes and parsley in bowl.

Place quail skin-side-down on bench, divide rice mixture between quail. Fold sides of quail over mixture, wrap quail in bacon, secure with toothpicks. Place quail on wire rack in roasting pan, brush with extra oil. Cook in covered barbeque or in 350°F oven about 25 minutes or until tender. Quail can also be cooked over coals; turn frequently during cooking. Serve quail with tomato sauce.

Tomato Sauce: Heat oil in pan, add onion and garlic, cook, stirring, until onion is soft. Add chili, undrained crushed tomatoes, paste, sugar and water. Bring to boil, sim-

mer, uncovered, about 15 minutes or until slightly thickened. Blend or process sauce until well combined.

Serves 8.

■ Quail can be prepared a day ahead. Sauce can be made a day ahead.
■ Storage: Covered, in refrigerator.
■ Freeze: Uncooked seasoned quail and cooked sauce suitable.
■ Microwave: Not suitable.

ABOVE: Clockwise from left: Garlic Apricot Chicken Wings, Fruity Quail with Bacon, Carrot and Pecan Turkey Roll.

BRANDY BUTTERED QUAIL

6 quail

FRUIT AND NUT SEASONING
½ cup chopped dried apricots
½ cup pitted prunes, chopped
¼ cup sliced almonds, toasted
1 tablespoon brandy
1½ cups cooked rice
2 green onions, chopped
**½ small chicken bouillon
    cube, crumbled**
1 egg, lightly beaten

BRANDY BUTTER
¼ cup (½ stick) butter, melted
2 teaspoons brandy

Bone quail following instructions in "Pre-Cooking Preparations" at the back of this book; leave legs and wings intact. Place quail skin-side-down on bench. Divide seasoning over quail, fold sides of quail over seasoning, secure with toothpicks; brush with brandy butter. Cook quail on barbeque or broil, turning frequently, until tender. Brush occasionally with remaining brandy butter during cooking. Quail can also be cooked in covered barbeque or in 350°F oven about 25 minutes or until quail is tender.

Fruit and Nut Seasoning: Place apricots in bowl, cover with hot water, stand 30 minutes. Drain apricots well, place in bowl, combine with remaining ingredients.

Brandy Butter: Combine butter and brandy in bowl.

Serves 6.

■ Quail can be prepared a day ahead.
■ Storage: Covered, in refrigerator.
■ Freeze: Uncooked seasoned
    quail suitable.
■ Microwave: Not suitable.

QUENELLE-FILLED CHICKEN BREASTS

8 chicken breast halves
2½ tablespoons butter, melted

QUENELLE
**1 boneless, skinless chicken breast
    half, chopped**
1 clove garlic, minced
2 teaspoons chopped fresh tarragon
⅓ cup heavy cream

BRANDY SAUCE
⅓ cup brandy
⅔ cup water
**2 large chicken bouillon
    cubes, crumbled**
**2½ tablespoons chopped
    fresh tarragon**
1 teaspoon lemon juice
⅓ cup heavy cream
2 teaspoons cornstarch
2 teaspoons water, extra

TANGY DUCK WITH ONIONS AND APPLE

4 boneless duck breast halves
1½ tablespoons cider vinegar
1½ tablespoons light soy sauce
1½ tablespoons dark brown sugar
1 apple
2½ tablespoons butter
2 onions, sliced
¼ teaspoon ground cinnamon

Trim excess fat from duck. Combine duck, vinegar, sauce and sugar in bowl, cover, refrigerate overnight, turning occasionally.

Cook duck on oiled barbeque plate or in pan about 4 minutes each side or until skin is well browned and duck is tender.

Peel and core apple, cut apple into thin wedges. Heat butter in pan, add onions, cook, stirring, until soft. Stir in apple, cook, covered, over low heat for 10 minutes, stirring occasionally. Stir in cinnamon, cook further 5 minutes; keep warm. Slice duck, serve over onion and apple mixture.

Serves 4.

■ Recipe can be prepared a day ahead.
■ Storage: Covered, in refrigerator.
■ Freeze: Uncooked marinated duck suitable.
■ Microwave: Not suitable.

LEFT: From left: Brandy Buttered Quail, Quenelle-Filled Chicken Breasts.
BELOW: Tangy Duck with Onions and Apple.

Loosen skin of chicken by sliding fingers between skin and meat, ensuring skin remains attached along 1 edge. Place rounded tablespoons of quenelle mixture under skin of each breast, press skin over quenelle, cover; refrigerate 1 hour.

Brush chicken with butter, cook on barbeque or broil, turning occasionally, until well browned and tender. Serve chicken with brandy sauce.

Quenelle: Blend or process chicken, garlic, tarragon and cream until smooth.

Brandy Sauce: Combine brandy, water, bouillon cubes, tarragon, juice and cream in pan. Stir over heat until boiling, stir in blended cornstarch and extra water. Stir over heat until sauce boils and thickens.

Serves 8.

■ Recipe can be prepared a day ahead.
■ Storage: Covered, in refrigerator.
■ Freeze: Prepared chicken suitable.
■ Microwave: Sauce suitable.

NUTTY CHICKEN PATTIES WITH MUSTARD BUTTER

2lb ground chicken
4 green onions, chopped
2 cloves garlic, minced
2½ tablespoons chopped fresh basil
1½ tablespoons chopped
   fresh rosemary
1 tablespoon chopped fresh oregano
1½ cups (3½oz) fresh bread crumbs
1 cup (4oz) chopped pistachios
1 tablespoon Worcestershire sauce
2 small chicken bouillon
   cubes, crumbled
2 teaspoons seeded mustard
1 egg, lightly beaten

MUSTARD BUTTER
5oz (1¼ sticks) butter
2 tablespoons seeded mustard

Process chicken with onions, garlic, and herbs until well combined. Transfer mixture to bowl, stir in bread crumbs, nuts, sauce, bouillon cubes, mustard and egg; mix well. Shape mixture into about 20 drumstick-shaped patties, cover, refrigerate 2 hours. Cook patties on oiled barbeque plate or in pan, turning occasionally, until cooked through. Serve with mustard butter.

Mustard Butter: Beat butter and mustard in bowl until combined.

Serves 6.

- ■ Recipe can be prepared a day ahead.
- ■ Storage: Covered, in refrigerator.
- ■ Freeze: Uncooked patties suitable.
- ■ Microwave: Not suitable.

CHICKEN AND CHEESE MUFFINS

1 tablespoon olive oil
1 onion, finely chopped
3 cups self-rising flour
2oz package cream of chicken dry
   soup mix
1 small chicken bouillon
   cube, crumbled
2 teaspoons sugar
1 teaspoon dried oregano leaves
2 teaspoons dried mixed herbs
½ cup grated fresh Parmesan cheese
1½ cups (10oz) finely chopped
   cooked chicken
2⅓ cups buttermilk
1 cup (¼lb) grated cheddar cheese

Grease 12 x ¾ cup muffin tins. Heat oil in pan, add onion, cook, stirring, until very soft; cool. Sift flour into large bowl. Add onion mixture, dry soup mix, bouillon cube, sugar, herbs, Parmesan cheese and chicken; mix well. Add buttermilk, stir until combined. Spoon mixture into prepared pans, sprinkle with cheddar cheese. Bake in 350°F oven about 45 minutes or until muffins are browned and cooked through.

Makes 12.

■ Muffins can be made a day ahead.
■ Storage: Covered, in refrigerator.
■ Freeze: Cooked muffins suitable.
■ Microwave: Not suitable.

QUAIL WITH FRESH RASPBERRY SAUCE

6 quail, halved
1½ tablespoons balsamic vinegar
2½ tablespoons dark brown sugar
1 tablespoon olive oil

RASPBERRY SAUCE
7oz raspberries
2½ tablespoons dry white wine
2 teaspoons chopped fresh basil
1 clove garlic, minced
½ teaspoon sugar

Combine quail, vinegar, sugar and oil in bowl, cover, refrigerate several hours or overnight, turning occasionally.

Cook quail on oiled barbeque plate or in pan about 10 minutes, turning occasionally, or until well browned and cooked through. Serve with sauce.

Raspberry Sauce: Blend or process berries and wine until smooth. Push through sieve to remove seeds. Combine berry puree with basil, garlic and sugar. Cover, stand 20 minutes before using.

Serves 6.

■ Recipe can be prepared 2 days ahead.
■ Storage: Covered, in refrigerator.
■ Freeze: Uncooked marinated quail suitable.
■ Microwave: Not suitable.

CRISPY CHICKEN WITH AVOCADO SAUCE

2½lb chicken thighs, boned, skinned
¾ cup white vinegar
4 cloves garlic, minced
1 small chicken bouillon cube, crumbled

AVOCADO SAUCE
1 avocado
2 teaspoons grated lime zest
2½ tablespoons lime juice
2½ tablespoons No-Oil herb and garlic dressing
2½ tablespoons olive oil

Cut chicken into thin strips, place in shallow dish; pour over combined vinegar, garlic and bouillon cube. Cover, refrigerate several hours or overnight.

Drain chicken; pat dry with absorbent paper. Cook chicken on oiled barbeque plate or in pan until chicken is tender. Serve with avocado sauce.

Avocado Sauce: Blend or process all ingredients until smooth.

Serves 6.

■ Chicken can be prepared a day ahead. Sauce best made just before serving.
■ Storage: Covered, in refrigerator.
■ Freeze: Not suitable.
■ Microwave: Not suitable.

LEFT: From top: Chicken and Cheese Muffins, Nutty Chicken Patties with Mustard Butter.
BELOW: From top: Quail with Fresh Raspberry Sauce, Crispy Chicken with Avocado Sauce.

CHILI CITRUS MARYLANDS

6 chicken marylands (thighs with legs)
½ cup concentrated orange juice
1½ tablespoons chili sauce
1 teaspoon grated lemon zest
½ teaspoon grated lime zest
1½ tablespoons lime juice
1 tablespoon brown vinegar
½ teaspoon dried thyme leaves
1 teaspoon cornstarch

Add marylands to pan of boiling water, boil, uncovered, 5 minutes; drain. Make 4 deep cuts in each maryland, place in dish, pour over combined concentrated juice, sauce, zests, lime juice, vinegar and thyme. Cover, refrigerate overnight.

Drain marylands; reserve marinade. Cook marylands on barbeque or broil until tender. Blend cornstarch with reserved marinade in pan. Stir over heat until sauce mixture boils and thickens. Serve sauce with marylands.

Serves 6.

- ■ Can be prepared 2 days ahead.
- ■ Storage: Covered, in refrigerator.
- ■ Freeze: Uncooked marinated marylands suitable.
- ■ Microwave: Not suitable.

HONEYED CHICKEN AND ORANGE PARCELS

¼ cup light soy sauce
¼ cup honey
4 boneless, skinless chicken breast halves
1 orange
1 red bell pepper
1 red onion, finely chopped
¼lb button mushrooms, sliced

Combine sauce and honey in pan, stir until just boiling. Brush chicken with honey mixture, cover, refrigerate 2 hours.

Using vegetable peeler, thinly cut peel from orange, cut peel into thin strips. Completely peel orange, cut orange into segments. Cut pepper into thin strips.

Just before serving, divide onion between 4 x 8 inch square pieces of foil, top with chicken, orange peel strips, orange segments, pepper and mushrooms. Fold foil to form parcels, cook on barbeque plate about 15 minutes or until tender. Parcels can also be cooked in 350°F oven or covered barbeque about 20 minutes or until tender.

Serves 4.

- ■ Chicken can be prepared 3 hours ahead.
- ■ Storage: Covered, in refrigerator.
- ■ Freeze: Not suitable.
- ■ Microwave: Not suitable.

ABOVE: From left: Honeyed Chicken and Orange Parcels, Chili Citrus Marylands. RIGHT: From top: Chestnut Macadamia Chicken, Tropical Turkey Kabobs with Mango Cream.

TROPICAL TURKEY KABOBS WITH MANGO CREAM

15oz can pineapple slices
2lb boneless, skinless turkey
breast half
1½ tablespoons lime juice
1 teaspoon cracked black
peppercorns
2 bananas, sliced
1½ large mangoes, roughly chopped
1 cup coconut
1 cup packaged ground almonds

MANGO CREAM
½ large mango, chopped
½ cup light sour cream
2 teaspoons chopped fresh chives

Drain pineapple, reserve ½ cup syrup. Cut turkey into bite-sized pieces. Combine turkey with reserved syrup, lime juice and peppercorns in bowl. Cover, refrigerate 3 hours or overnight.

Drain turkey, reserve marinade. Cut pineapple slices into quarters. Thread turkey, pineapple, banana and mango onto skewers.

Cook kabobs on barbeque or broil, brushing with reserved marinade until turkey is tender. Sprinkle with combined coconut and almonds just before serving. Serve with mango cream.

Mango Cream: Blend or process mango and cream until smooth. Stir in chives.

Makes about 24.

- Recipe can be prepared a day ahead.
- Storage: Covered, in refrigerator.
- Freeze: Uncooked marinated turkey suitable.
- Microwave: Not suitable.

CHESTNUT MACADAMIA CHICKEN

8oz can chestnut spread
⅓ cup seasoned stuffing mix
¼ cup chopped macadamia nuts
8 chicken breast halves
8 thick slices bacon

APRICOT SAUCE
2 teaspoons cornstarch
¼ teaspoon ground gingerroot
1 cup apricot nectar

Combine spread, stuffing mix and nuts in bowl. Gently loosen skin from chicken by pushing fingers between skin and meat to form a pocket. Push chestnut mixture under skin, wrap each breast in bacon, secure with small skewers or toothpicks. Cook chicken on barbeque or broil until well browned and cooked through. Serve chicken with apricot sauce.

Apricot Sauce: Blend cornstarch and gingerroot with a little of the nectar in pan, stir in remaining nectar. Stir over heat until sauce boils and thickens, boil 1 minute.

Serves 8.

- Recipe can be prepared a day ahead.
- Storage: Covered, in refrigerator.
- Freeze: Uncooked seasoned chicken suitable.
- Microwave: Sauce suitable.

PRE-COOKING PREPARATIONS

Experiment a little and soon you'll be boning and preparing chicken and more in style, but don't worry if at first yours don't look quite like ours; it's only a matter of practice. This section also contains a guide to cuts we bought; however, you may find these vary according to where you shop. We've also included cooking and microwaving tips to help you get top results with this book.

You can buy fresh or frozen poultry, but be sure frozen poultry is completely thawed before cooking. Remove any remaining feathers, wash bird inside and out, remove neck and any giblets (heart, liver and gizzard) left inside. Pat the bird dry inside and out with absorbent paper.

Tuck any neck flap under, tie legs together, tuck wings under (see "How to Truss a Bird").

When halving small birds such as quail or Rock Cornish hens, the backbone can be removed to make the serving more attractive, unless otherwise stated in recipes.

We bought whole birds and cuts, etc., that were readily available. Giblets were removed; neck was sometimes left in; check label for details.

Quail and pheasant are widely available or can be obtained from a game shop. Various turkey cuts are also widely available now.

We show you how to bone a bird, but sometimes the butcher or poultry shop will have boned birds available or will bone a bird for you.. Poultry cuts, etc., may vary according to the supplier but here's what we used.

WHAT WE BOUGHT

CHICKEN BREAST: has fillets, skin and bones.

CHICKEN THIGH CUTLET: has skin; has 1 bone in the center; is sometimes referred to as a chicken chop.

CHICKEN WINGS: have skin and bones; a little meat.

BONELESS, SKINLESS CHICKEN BREASTS OR HALVES: have skin and bones removed, leaving the chicken fillet.

BONELESS DUCK BREAST: ours had a tiny portion of wings remaining and a large area of skin and fat attached; see Duck with Garlic Chicken Seasoning, page 44.

DRUMMETTES: we bought skinned drumsticks with the end of the bone chopped off; these are sometimes known as "lovely legs". The poultry shop may prepare them for you.

BONELESS DUCK BREAST HALVES: with or without skin and fat, no bone.

MARYLAND: leg and thigh are attached; has skin and bones.

OVEN-ROASTED TURKEY BREAST ROLL: is pressed into a roll; already cooked for convenience.

PHEASANT: game bird about 2lb.

QUAIL: small game birds from about ½lb to ¾lb.

BONELESS QUAIL BREAST HALVES: Single breasts with skin; the packet we bought contained 6 breast halves.

ROCK CORNISH HEN: very young chicken (poussin); usually from ½lb to 1¼lb.

SELF-BASTING TURKEY: is slightly different from a regular turkey, and you should follow package instructions for thawing and preparation. ("Self-basting" means the breast of a chicken or turkey has been injected with a tasty blend of ingredients to add flavor and keep the bird moist during cooking.) Some self-basting turkeys come with a pop-up timer to tell you when the bird is cooked through.

SIZES: Whole birds usually have number and weight on packaging; our recipes give the weight for easy buying as packaging varies.

BONELESS TURKEY BREAST: small or large piece cut from the breast meat.

TURKEY BUFFE: fresh or frozen whole breast on the bone; has skin.

COOKING TIPS

- To prevent over-browning when baking, cover legs, wings and breast (or whole bird) with foil if browning too quickly.
- Don't baste too often unless specified in recipe. Frequent basting keeps the skin moist and you may not get the brown, crisp skin you want. As well, the temperature keeps dropping when you open the oven door.
- Roasting a chicken is generally straightforward, put it on a wire rack in the roasting pan or put it straight into the roasting pan, cook for time required, watch for over-browning, and the chicken will be great; follow individual recipes.
- Duck is very fatty and skin should be pricked all over to release the fat during cooking. Be careful to prick skin only, not down into the meat, otherwise juices could run out and the duck meat will be dry. Prick once or twice more during cooking, or as specified in recipe.

  When roasting, place duck on wire rack in roasting pan and add about half a cup of water to the pan to stop the fat spattering. A lot of fat and liquid will drain into the dish so handle the dish with care when removing it from the oven.
- Cooking a goose is similar to a duck; again prick only the skin, not through to the meat.
- Cooking a turkey is different, because turkey meat is dry and tends to dry out further during cooking. Don't prick skin unless specified in recipe. Add about half a cup of water to roasting pan as this helps to keep the turkey moist.
- Cooking Rock Cornish hens and quail is quite quick, but watch them as they can easily brown and burn. Cover with foil as above.

HOW TO TRUSS A BIRD

Trussing means to secure poultry or game with kitchen string or skewers so that it will keep its shape during cooking. It's optional, but it does make poultry look nicer for serving, and it's what we mean when we say "tie legs together, tuck wings under". Here's how to do it:

1: Tie kitchen string around tail end of bird, then around legs, bringing string between legs and body towards wings.

2: Wrap kitchen string around wings, turn bird over, tie string firmly between wings.

HOW TO CUT CHICKEN PIECES

Some recipes in our book specify chicken pieces; these can be bought ready-jointed or, if you prefer, you can joint a chicken yourself. A jointed chicken separates into 9 pieces: 2 legs, 2 thighs, 2 wings, 2 breasts, 1 back. The back is not considered an individual serving portion, but can be use to accompany another portion, such as a wing, or used to make soup.

1: Cut thigh and leg portions from chicken. Separate legs and thighs.

2: Cut wing portions from chicken.

3: Using poultry shears, cut backbone section from chicken.

4: Cut breast section in half.

5: The chicken is now in 9 portions.

HOW TO CHOP CHICKEN CHINESE-STYLE

For Chinese chicken dishes, chicken is cut into smaller pieces than for most other recipes. Here's the way to cut the chicken, using poultry shears (or scissors) and a cleaver:

1: Place chicken on board, breast-side-up. Cut through breastbone, a little to 1 side, and right through backbone.

2: Cut both pieces of chicken in half.

3: Now cut between each wing and breast, cutting through joint. Cut or chop between each leg and thigh. You should have 8 pieces.

4: Chop each wing into 3 pieces. Chop each leg into 3 pieces. Chop each breast into 3 pieces. Chop each thigh into 3 pieces. You should have 24 pieces, as pictured above.

HOW TO BONE OUT A CHICKEN

To "bone out" a bird, you remove the bones so the bird can be seasoned and rolled or whatever is specified. Here, we show you how to bone out a chicken for Chicken with Red Peppers on page 46, but the guidelines apply to any bird.

1: Using a sharp knife, cut off wing tips at the second joint. Cut through skin of chicken along center back. Using tip of knife, separate flesh from backbone on 1 side of chicken, cutting through thigh joint, then, following the shape of the bones, gradually ease flesh away from bone. Holding rib cage away from chicken, carefully cut the breast flesh away from the bone, cutting through wing joint.

2: Hold up 1 thigh with 1 hand. To remove flesh, cut around top of bone, scrape down bone to next joint, cut around flesh again, scrape down to the end. Pull bone out and cut away. Repeat boning process with other half of chicken. Turn flesh of thighs and wings inside chicken.

3: Spoon seasoning down center of chicken (over prosciutto here, or as specified in recipe). Fold 1 side of chicken over seasoning, then fold over other side to overlap by about ¾ inch.

4: Sew overlapped edges together using a needle and dark thread (dark so it is easy to see for removal later). Tie chicken with kitchen string to keep shape during cooking. Then follow individual recipe to cook and serve.

HOW TO BONE OUT A QUAIL

A quail is such a tiny bird that it is best handled as follows. Leave legs and wings intact, or as recipe specifies:

1: Using sharp knife, cut along each side of quail backbone; remove and discard backbone.

2: Place quail skin-side-down on board. Carefully cut through thigh joints and wing joints without cutting skin. Scrape meat away from rib cage.

3: Continue scraping meat from rib cage and breastbone; remove and discard bones. Quail is ready to fill with seasoning. Wings should then be tucked under and legs tied together with kitchen string; cover legs with foil during cooking to prevent buring.

MICROWAVING POULTRY

Poultry generally is suitable to cook in the microwave oven. However, some points should be considered. Poultry will not brown well when cooked in the microwave oven, and therefore won't look like our photographs. Some "cosmetic touches" can be used. Soy sauce, tomato ketchup, paprika, honey, marmalades, jams, etc., can be used to add color.
A browning dish can also be used for pieces of poultry to add color.
Small turkeys, up to about 7lb, buffes and turkey pieces can be cooked in the microwave. Larger turkeys won't cook through evenly and some don't fit in the oven!
Duck, pheasant and goose would not be suitable in the microwave – the meat would be quite tough and the fat would not become crisp.
Cover the legs and wings of whole chickens, Rock Cornish hens, quail and small turkeys firmly with aluminum foil to prevent overcooking. A narrow strip of foil can be placed along breastbone to prevent drying out. Chicken, Rock Cornish hens and quail can be cooked on HIGH power (100%). Turkey would be best cooked on MEDIUM HIGH or MEDIUM to prevent drying out.

CUP & SPOON MEASUREMENTS

To ensure accuracy in your recipes use standard measuring equipment.
a) 8 fluid oz cup for measuring liquids.
b) a graduated set of four cups – measuring 1 cup, half, third and quarter cup – for items such as flour, sugar, etc.
When measuring in these fractional cups level off at the brim.
c) a graduated set of five spoons: tablespoon (½ fluid oz liquid capacity), teaspoon, half, quarter and eighth teaspoons.
All spoon measurements are level.
We have used large eggs with an average weight of 2oz each in all our recipes.

GLOSSARY

Here are some terms, names and alternatives to help everyone use and understand our recipes perfectly.

ALCOHOL: is optional but gives special flavor. You can use fruit juice or water instead to make up the liquid content in our recipes.

ALL-SPICE: pimento in ground form.

ALMONDS

GROUND: we used commercially ground, packaged almonds.

SLIVERED: almonds cut into slivers.

SLICED: almonds cut into thin slices.

BACON SLICES: we used thick slices where specified.

BAMBOO SKEWERS: can be used instead of metal skewers if they are soaked in water overnight or several hours beforehand to prevent burning during cooking. They are available in several different lengths.

BEAN SPROUTS: we used mung bean sprouts; these are available fresh or canned in brine.

BELL PEPPERS: capsicums.

BREAD CRUMBS

PACKAGED: use fine packaged, unseasoned bread crumbs.

FRESH: use fresh bread 1- or 2-day-old bread crumbs made by grating, blending or processing.

BOUILLON CUBES: available in beef, chicken and vegetable. As a guide, use 1 large crumbled bouillon cube to every 2 cups water. These cubes contain salt, so allow for this when seasoning food.

BOUILLON, INSTANT: can be used instead of cubes; a small cube is equivalent to 1 tablespoon instant bouillon.

BOUQUET GARNI: generally consists of a bay leaf, a sprig of fresh thyme, and several parsley sprigs tied together at the stems with cotton or thin string to make removal easier at the end of cooking time. When dried herbs are used it is best to tie them in a piece of muslin (see picture following Parsley, Flat-Leafed).

BUTTER: use salted or unsalted (sweet) butter.

BUTTERMILK: is now made by adding a culture to skim milk to give a slightly acid flavor; skim milk can be substituted.

CABANOSSI: a type of ready-to-eat sausage; also known as cabana.

1. Chinese dried pork sausage. 2. Chorizo sausage. 3. Cabanossi. 4. Prosciutto. 5. Pastrami. 6. Pancetta.

CHEESE

BLUE VEIN: white cheese with distinctive blue veins and a tangy sharp flavor.

BOCCONCINI: small balls of mild delicate cheese packaged in water or whey to keep them white and soft. The water should be just milky and cheese should be white; yellowing indicates that it's stale.

COTTAGE: soft, unripened mild-tasting curd cheese of different fat content from skim milk to full-cream milk.

CHEDDAR: use a firm good-tasting cheddar.

CREAM CHEESE: unripened, smooth, spreadable cheese.

FETA: is cured and stored in brine; has white or pale cream color with a soft to firm open texture and acidic, salty taste.

MOZZARELLA: a fresh, semi-soft cheese with a delicate, clean, fresh curd taste; has a low melting point and stringy texture when heated.

PARMESAN: sharp-tasting cheese used as a flavor accent. We prefer to use fresh Parmesan cheese; however, it is available already finely grated.

PECORINO: hard cheese with grainy texture and sharp-tangy flavor.

RICOTTA: a fresh, unripened light curd cheese of rich flavor.

CHESTNUT SPREAD: canned sweetened chestnut puree.

CHICKEN SEASONING: packaged mix of herbs and spices, salt, sugar, natural chicken extract, etc., used to accentuate flavor.

CHICORY: a curly-leafed vegetable, mainly used in salads.

1. Boston lettuce. 2. Radicchio lettuce. 3. Chicory.
4. Iceberg lettuce. 5. Oak leaf lettuce (red).
6. Red leaf lettuce. 7. Oak leaf lettuce (green).

CHILIES: are available in many different types and sizes. The small ones (bird's eye or bird peppers) are the hottest. Use tight rubber gloves when chopping fresh chilies as they can burn your skin. The seeds are the hottest part of the chilies so remove them if you want to reduce heat content of recipes.

1. Red bell pepper. 2. Green bell pepper.
3. Yellow bell pepper. 4. Red chili peppers.
5. Green chili peppers.

CHILI POWDER: ground dried chilies.

CHILI SAUCE: we used a hot or sweet Chinese variety. It consists of chilies, salt and vinegar. We used it sparingly so that you can easily increase amounts in recipes to suit your taste.

CHINESE BARBEQUED DUCK: can be bought ready to eat from speciality Chinese food stores.

CHINESE MIXED PICKLES: consists of fruit and vegetables which are preserved in vinegar, sugar and salt. The ingredients in the jar we used were gingerroot, green onions, papaya, cucumbers, carrots, chili and pears.

CHINESE RICE WINE: available from speciality Chinese food stores. Use dry sherry, if preferred.

CHORIZO SAUSAGE: Spanish and Mexican highly spiced pork sausage seasoned with garlic, cayenne pepper, chili, etc. They are ready to eat when bought. If unavailable, use a spicy salami. See picture under Cabanossi.

CILANTRO: also known as Chinese parsley or coriander. The leaves, roots and stems can be used.

COCONUT CREAM: use the unsweetened variety available in cans and cartons in supermarkets and Asian food stores; coconut milk can be substituted, although it is not as thick.

COCONUT MILK: use unsweetened variety if bought, but it is also easy to make using desiccated coconut. (Coconut milk is not the liquid inside the mature coconut.) Place 2 cups desiccated coconut in large bowl, cover with 2½ cups hot water, cover, stand until mixture is just warm. Mix with the hand, then strain through fine sieve or cloth, squeezing out as much liquid as you can. This will give you about 1½ cups thick milk; it can be used when canned coconut cream is specified. The same coconut can be used again; simply add another 2½ cups hot water, and continue as above, this will give you a watery milk. It can be combined with the first, thicker milk and is a good substitute for the unsweetened, canned coconut milk specified in our recipes. It can be blended or processed for about 20 seconds, then strained as directed above.

COCONUT, SHREDDED: thin strips of dried coconut.

CORNMEAL: ground corn (maize); is similar to yellow cornmeal but paler yellow in color and finer. One cannot be substituted for the other as cooking times will vary.

CORNMEAL, YELLOW: usually made from ground corn (maize); is similar to cornmeal but is coarser and darker. One cannot be substituted for the other as cooking times will vary.

1. Cornmeal. 2. Yellow cornmeal.

CREAM

HALF AND HALF: thin pouring cream.

HEAVY: use when specified.

WHIPPING: is specified when necessary in recipes.

LIGHT SOUR: a less dense commercially

cultured soured cream; do not substitute this for sour cream.

SOUR: a thick commercially cultured soured cream.

CREME DE CACAO: chocolate-flavored liqueur.

CREME DE CASSIS: blackcurrant-flavored liqueur.

CURRY POWDER: a convenient combination of spices in powdered form. Curry powder consists of chili, coriander, cumin, fennel, fenugreek and turmeric in varying proportions.

DILL PICKLE: pickled baby cucumber.

EGG ROLL SKINS: are sold frozen, thaw before using, keep covered with a damp cloth while using.

FISH SAUCE: an essential ingredient in the cooking of a number of South East Asian countries, including Thailand and Vietnam. It is made from the liquid drained from salted, fermented anchovies. It has a strong smell and taste. Use sparingly.

FIVE-SPICE POWDER: a pungent mixture of ground spices which includes cinnamon, cloves, fennel, star anise and Szechuan peppers.

FLOUR

ALL-PURPOSE FLOUR: use when specified.

SELF-RISING FLOUR: substitute all-purpose flour and baking powder in the proportions of ¾ metric cup all-purpose flour to 2 level teaspoons of baking powder. Sift together several times before using.

GARAM MASALA: there are many variations of the combinations of cardamom, cinnamon, cloves, coriander, cumin and nutmeg used to make up this spice used often in Indian cooking. Sometimes pepper is used to make a hot variation. Garam masala is readily available in jars.

GARLIC: strong-scented pungent bulb with a distinctive taste. Bulb contains cloves; use number of cloves specified in individual recipes.

GINGER ALE: ginger beer.

GINGERROOT, FRESH OR GREEN: scrape away outside skin and grate, chop or slice gingerroot as required. Fresh, peeled gingerroot can be preserved with enough dry sherry to cover; keep in jar in refrigerator; it will keep for months.

GROUND: is also available but should not be substituted for fresh gingerroot.

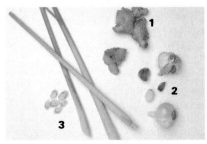

1. Gingerroot. 2. Garlic. 3. Lemon grass.

GINGER WINE: an Australian-made alcoholic sweet wine infused with finely

ground gingerroot. If unavailable, substitute ginger ale.

GRAND MARNIER: an orange-flavored liqueur. Cointreau can be substituted.

HERBS: we have specified when to use fresh or dried herbs. We used dried (not ground) herbs in the proportion of 1:4 for fresh herbs; for example, 1 teaspoon dried herbs instead of 4 teaspoons chopped fresh herbs.

HOISIN SAUCE: a thick sweet Chinese barbeque sauce made from salted black beans, onions and garlic.

HORSERADISH CREAM: paste of horseradish, oil, mustard and flavorings.

JAM: conserve.

LARD: fat obtained from melting down and clarifying pork fat; available packaged from supermarkets and butchers.

LEMON CURD: lemon cheese or lemon butter available in jars.

LEMON GRASS: needs to be bruised or chopped before using. It will keep in a jug of water at room temperature for several weeks; the water must be changed daily. It can be bought dried. To reconstitute: place several pieces of dried lemon grass in a bowl; cover with hot water, stand 20 minutes; drain. This amount is a substitute for 1 stalk of fresh lemon grass.

MINT JELLY: vinegar-based jelly usually served with lamb.

MUSHROOMS: we used different types of mushrooms, see picture below.

CHINESE DRIED: unique in flavor; soak in boiling water, covered, for 20 minutes, drain. Remove and discard stems, use caps as indicated in recipes.

1. Chinese dried mushrooms. 2. Fresh cap mushrooms. 3. Black fungus. 4. Fresh button mushrooms.

MUSTARD, SEEDED: a French style of mustard with crushed mustard seeds.

MUSTARD SEEDS: tiny seeds used in curries, pickling and mustard; seeds can be black (spicy and piquant), brown (less piquant) or white (milder in flavor).

OIL: we used polyunsaturated vegetable oil unless otherwise specified.

OLIVE: we used a virgin olive oil but use the grade you prefer. Olive oil comes in several different grades with each grade having a different flavor. The most flavorsome is the extra virgin variety usually used in home-made dressings. Extra virgin olive oil is the purest quality oil. Virgin oil is obtained from the pulp of high-grade fruit. Pure olive oil is pressed from the pulp and kernels of second grade olives. Extra light olive oil is lighter in color and flavor to pure and virgin.

SESAME: made from roasted, crushed white sesame seeds. It is always used in small quantities. Do not use for frying.

ONION, GREEN: also known as spring onion or scallion.

ONION, RED: red-skinned, pink-fleshed variety, almost odorless and popular in salads.

1. Leeks. 2. Green onions. 3. Red onions.

OYSTER-FLAVORED SAUCE: a rich brown sauce made from oysters cooked in salt and soy sauce, then thickened with different types of starches.

PANCETTA: Italian in origin, is ready-to-eat spicy processed meat made from pork belly which has been salted and cured.

PARSLEY, FLAT-LEAFED: readily available popular herb also known as continental or Italian parsley.

1. Flat-leafed parsley. 2. Fresh bouquet garni.
3. Dried bouquet garni.

PASTRAMI: highly seasoned smoked beef ready to eat when bought.

PEPPER, SEASONED: a combination of pepper, red bell pepper, garlic flakes, paprika and natural chicken extract.

PIMIENTOS (sweet red peppers): are preserved in brine in cans or jars.

PLUM SAUCE: a dipping sauce which consists of plums preserved in vinegar, sweetened with sugar and flavored with chilies and spices.

PROSCIUTTO: ready-to-eat uncooked, unsmoked ham cured in salt.

RICE

BASMATI: similar appearance to long-grain rice with a fine aroma. It is grown in the foothills of the Himalayas. Basmati rice

should be washed thoroughly in several changes of water before being cooked. Cook as ordinary rice.

WILD: from North America, it is not a member of the rice family, it is expensive as it is difficult to cultivate but has a distinctive nutty flavor.

LONG-GRAIN: elongated grains.

1. Wild rice. 2. Short-grain rice. 3. Long-grain rice.
4. Basmati rice.

SAFFRON: the most expensive of all spices, is available in threads or ground form. It is made from the dried stamens of the crocus flower.

SAKE: Japan's favorite rice wine; is used in cooking, marinading and as part of dipping sauces. Dry sherry, vermouth or brandy can be substituted.

SAMBAL OELEK: a paste made from ground chilies and salt.

SEASONED STUFFING MIX: a tasty, packaged mix containing bread crumbs and flavorings.

SNOW PEAS: also known as Chinese pea pods.

Snow peas.

SOY SAUCE: made from fermented soy beans. The light sauce is generally used with white meat, the darker variety with red meat. There is a multi-purpose salt-reduced sauce available, also Japanese soy sauce. It is a matter of personal taste which sauce you use.

SPINACH: a soft-leaved vegetable, more delicate in taste than Swiss chard; however, young Swiss chard can be substituted.

STAR ANISE: the dried star-shaped fruit of an evergreen tree. It is used sparingly in

Chinese cooking and has a definite aniseed flavor.

SUGAR: use ordinary white sugar unless otherwise specified.

BROWN: use dark or light as specified.

SWEET POTATO: we used the orange-colored firm-textured sweet potato, unless otherwise specified.

SWISS CHARD: remove coarse white stems, cook green leafy parts as individual recipes indicate.

SZECHUAN PEPPERS: a mixture of different types of dried peppers, available from Asian food stores.

TOMATO

KETCHUP: use tomato ketchup.

SUN-DRIED: are dried tomatoes sometimes bottled in oil.

PASTE: a concentrated tomato puree used in flavoring soups, stews, sauces, etc.

PUREE: canned, pureed tomatoes (not tomato paste). Use fresh, peeled, pureed tomatoes as a substitute, if preferred.

SUPREME: a canned product consisting of tomatoes, onions, celery, bell peppers and various seasonings.

VINEGAR: we used both white and brown (malt) vinegar in this book.

BALSAMIC: originated in the province of Modena, Italy. Regional wine is specially processed then aged in antique wooden casks to give pungent flavor.

CIDER: mild vinegar made from fermented apples.

RED WINE: made from red wine, often flavored with herbs.

WINE: we used good-quality dry white and red wines.

WONTON SKINS: are thin squares or rounds of fresh noodle dough, available from Asian food stores. Use egg pastry sheets if unavailable.

1. Egg roll skins. 2. Wonton skins. 3. Fresh egg noodles. 4. Chinese dried noodles. 5. Gow gees pastry.

ZEST: colored skin of citrus fruit.

INDEX

Home Library

Salads

Sensational recipes for all occasions

Home Library

COUNTRY COOKING

Home Library

Healthy Heart Cookbook

LOWER CHOLESTEROL TOO!

Home Library

VEGETARIAN COOKING

THE BEST

Home Library

SEAFOOD RECIPES

Home Library

Italian COOKING CLASS COOKBOOK

Home Library

CHICKEN COOKBOOK

PLUS duck, quail, turkey, goose and more

Home Library

PASTA COOKBOOK

More than 170 recipes

Home Library

CHINESE COOKING CLASS COOKBOOK

Home Library

STARTERS AND SOUPS

Home Library

BEGINNERS' COOKBOOK

Home Library

FINGER FOOD

Best ever party food
Tempting hot and cold savouries
Do ahead and freezing tips